One Girl's War

JOAN MILLER

ONE GIRL'S WAR

PERSONAL EXPLOITS IN MI5's MOST SECRET STATION

BRANDON

First published 1986
Brandon Book Publishers Ltd,
Dingle, Co. Kerry

Paperback edition December 1986

Typesetting by Setleaders Ltd, Dublin
Printed and bound in the Republic of Ireland by
Mount Salus Press Ltd,
Folio House, Bishop Street, Dublin 8.

Contents

Behind Prison Bars

AT THE beginning of September 1939, I was on holiday in Sark. When I heard over the wireless that a declaration of war was imminent, I packed my bags, made my way to Guernsey and waited there to embark for Weymouth. While I waited, I wandered along to visit a fortune-teller, known to me from the previous year, who used a grubby pack of cards to predict the future. On this occasion, she told me that I would shortly find myself behind bars. My horror at this announcement must have been apparent, for she went on to assure me I wasn't due for a spell of imprisonment. But she was adamant that the image she described to me, prisoners exercising in a prison yard, indicated something about my life in the near future.

The first time I'd seen this woman, in the summer of 1938, she told me I was about to meet a naval officer – 'tall and fair' was how she described him – who would confide to me the story of his life, mentioning his strange childhood and his infatuation with a married woman, older than himself; this officer, according to the fortune-teller, would eventually become my husband. The wedding ring was clearly visible to her, she said, and she remarked on the absence of an engagement ring. I *did* meet such a person a few days later, as it happened, at a party on board the battleship *Nelson* which was showing the flag and was moored in St Peter Port, Guernsey, and, true enough, I became engaged to him, though the engagement didn't last at this particular time. I broke it off because Tom *would* get involved with other girls whenever he was away from me for any length of time, however often and however sincerely he promised not to. It didn't seem to augur well for a permanent relationship. However, on account of her near-accuracy, as I thought, about the business, I had a good deal of faith in this particular clairvoyant, and I couldn't help worrying about her reference to 'prison bars'.

We were already at war when I got back to my tiny Chelsea flat, after travelling to Weymouth by packet boat and then taking a train for London. It was Sunday, 3 September. I switched on the wireless and heard Mr Chamberlain's distinctive voice proclaiming our country's support for freedom and justice, and all the endangered qualities that shaped our way of life. It was impossible not to feel exhilarated, even while you remembered his earlier assurances of peace.

Soon afterwards came the first air-raid warning; it was a false alarm, but nevertheless eerie in the extreme. Later, the King told the nation in a broadcast that it was perhaps the most fateful moment in our history. Certainly everyone was keyed up to expect instant alarm and drama. I knew my own circumstances were about to change. When I looked through my letters, I found a telegram instructing me to be at the request stop opposite the Natural History Museum in South Kensington at nine a.m. the following morning. There, I was to board an unnumbered bus which I would find waiting. The telegram was signed 'Room 005'.

Some months earlier I had attended an interview at the War office and been pronounced suitable for employment there in the event of war. At the time I was working in the Display department of Elizabeth Arden's cosmetic firm in Bond Street. My first job, when I left boarding-school at sixteen, had been in an Andover tea-shop; this lasted until my mother, back in England on a visit from South Africa where she lived with her second husband, suddenly noticed what I was doing and decided it didn't accord at all with the social status she had acquired. (She had started out as a chorus girl from Dunbar, but married first into a rich Anglo-Portuguese family – my father's – and then ran off with an impeccably middle-class engineer attached to the Sudan Cotton Plantation.) I was whisked off to London and introduced to the chairman of Elizabeth Arden,* a friend and admirer of my mother's, who agreed to take me on as office girl. Having done her duty by me, my mother kissed me, gave me some cast-off clothes – mostly Worth or Chanel, it's true – and left for Marseilles, en route for the Sudan. I didn't see her again until the end of the war.

My starting wage at Elizabeth Arden's was £2 10s a week. Board and lodging in a hostel at Earls Court cost £2, and the rest went on fares, coffee and a sandwich at lunchtime. When I hired a typewriter at a weekly rate of 5s I had to go

---

* Interestingly enough, Elizabeth Arden's London head office, without the knowledge of the management, was used as a pre-war rendezvous point by the Gestapo.

without the sandwich. However, I succeeded in teaching myself to type and this got me into the Advertising department and then into Display. Some of my duties here were more taxing than others. I remember once hanging upside down in a window of Selfridge's store in Oxford Street, trying to make an arrangement of some jars of bath salts and soaps in a deep-sea setting, while the proprietor – the redoubtable Mr Selfridge himself, in frock coat, striped trousers and high stiff collar – strode up and down admonishing me. 'Hurry up, young lady,' he said. 'Do you not realize that the loss in sales whenever a window is closed off amounts to £11 a minute?' That seemed a huge amount to me at the time – the thought of it made me a great deal more nervous.

London was a strange place to live and work during those years. As the 1930s wore on, the sense of an approaching war made many people apprehensive; but something remained of the gaiety that had characterized the previous decade. My generation – those born at the end of the earlier war – was particularly insouciant, I think, few of us being sufficiently sanguine to attach much importance to Chamberlain's slogan, 'Peace in our time'. While we had peace, though, we were anxious to make the most of it.

In the autumn of 1938 I received a series of letters from my mother, who wanted to know what part I intended to play in the coming war. Her friends' daughters, she told me, were all enlisting in the Women's Services, becoming trainee nurses and VADs, or preparing to work in Service canteens. Where did that leave me? Behaving selfishly as usual, she supposed. She was sure I was deficient in patriotic instincts. Her attitude, unduly critical as ever, depressed and irritated me – all the more so since her accusations in this instance weren't ill-founded. It was true I hadn't given much thought to the question of finding creditable employment in the event of a national emergency. Now that I did think about it, I quickly rejected the idea of joining the WRNS or the WAAF; my temperament, I decided, was wrong for the regimentation I imagined that course of action would entail.

How was I to satisfy my mother and stop her pestering me with letters? This worry was at the front of my mind when I arranged to have supper with an old school friend, Janet Withers. Janet, who worked in the War Office, proved unexpectedly helpful, offering to recommend me for a job similar to hers. Without having a clear idea of what her work involved, I agreed. Before we parted that evening she advised me to include shorthand among my accomplishments. Never mind that it wasn't true – the alternative was to get stuck in the Registry (MI5's filing department) along with her. I knew virtually no shorthand, but I was prepared to bluff my way through.

My social standing was in my favour, I suppose, and so were the references I was able to supply from two top-ranking Service officers (one in my own family and one a friend) and from the Dame of Sark. These, together with my supposed proficiency in shorthand and typing, were sufficient to get me listed as a potential recruit for MI5. I was interviewed by Miss Dicker, who was then in charge of the female staff, and warned that I would be summoned by telegram as soon as war broke out. I believed, in common with nearly everyone else, that it would only be a matter of months.

Now the telegram had come and I set out as directed, suffering some trepidation over the way I had misrepresented my secretarial abilities, but otherwise in high spirits. The 'mystery tour' aspect of Room 055's instructions appealed to my sense of adventure. I was twenty-one, happy, without personal ties, and ready to make the most of any experience that came my way. I wasn't sorry that a whole section of my life was over; elation and nervousness left no room for any other feeling.

I found the bus parked opposite the Natural History Museum. Some girls like myself were already on board, all got up, like me, in the ex-private schoolgirl's daytime uniform – grey flannel skirt, lambswool jersey and single string of pearls. A couple of youngish men in bowler hats, reading newspapers, sat near the front. Nobody spoke. Ignorance of the correct way to behave, and unwillingness to admit it, I suppose, kept us all unnaturally silent as the bus whizzed along. Where were we heading for? I soon found out, and, as I did, I gained an inkling of what the Guernsey fortune-teller's prediction had meant. The bus had drawn up outside Wormwood Scrubs.

I didn't know it at the time, but Sir Vernon Kell, Director-General of MI5 had arranged earlier in the year for a transfer of the Security Service from its cramped offices in Thames House, Millbank, and Horseferry Road, SW1, to His Majesty's Prison at Wormwood Scrubs, should war break out. At the beginning of September the evacuation of prisoners was still going on, and among those left behind, and exercising in the yard, one girl espied her father's ex-lawyer (so the rumour went). By now a certain amount of chattering and exclaiming was taking place around me for all the world as if we were assembling in a school hall at the start of a new term. It was rather disorientating, I must say; but I wasn't too bemused to notice the state of confusion that prevailed. Prisoners' cells had been converted into makeshift offices, but, with so many new arrivals milling about the place, it was proving difficult to get everyone settled, let alone provided with a proper staff. Taking my turn with the other girls, I waited to see Miss Dicker, hoping I would be assigned to a job not wildly unsuitable. I wasn't surprised to find this agreeable and efficient lady looking somewhat harassed, and I applauded the way she gave me her full attention while I began to confess that my shorthand probably wasn't up to standard. Before she could answer, however, the telephone rang. Even from where I sat, I could tell the call was coming from someone in an indignant and agitated state. 'Yes, Lord

Cottenham,' Miss Dicker said in a soothing manner, 'I have a Miss Miller with me at the moment, a very nice and experienced girl, and I will send her along to your cell. I think she will suit you.'

Motor-racing was one of my great enthusiasms and I had often watched Lord Cottenham race at Brooklands. I managed to locate his cell, ruefully wondering what my experience was supposed to consist of, and recognized him at once. At the time this peer of the realm was about thirty-eight, blue-eyed, with receding reddish hair, and always sported well-cut, eccentric clothes. He took one look at me and said, 'Thank God. Get rid of that other girl and come back straight away. She is having hysterics in the next cell.' Poor girl, she was certainly showing signs of distress, standing in the middle of a jumble of papers and moaning, 'I can't do it. I really can't.' I sent her off with false assurances that something else less onerous had been found for her, thereby commending myself to Lord Cottenham who thought this showed great presence of mind. He commended himself to me by not making a fuss about my lack of shorthand. 'I couldn't care less,' he said.

My new boss was in charge of MI5's transport section (under Major Malcolm Cumming), responsible for sending out despatch riders bearing top-secret communications, issuing petrol coupons and arranging transport for those in important offices. These duties were soon delegated to me. I shared a cell with another young motor-racing champion, Jock Horsfall, now one of MI5's chief drivers. This state of affairs, happy enough if not very exciting, lasted for a couple of months.

During this time I got to know Sir Vernon Kell, the Director-General, who took a personal interest in everyone on his staff. 'You must come to dinner with my wife and myself,' he said one day. So I visited them at their house, and learnt from Sir Vernon the proper attitude to take to people who persisted in enquiring about my job. 'Say you work for MI5,' he told me. 'Then, if they try to cross-question you, you will know they are wrong somehow.' I was introduced to their son, who took me out once or twice; I remember going with him to L'Escargot, in Soho, and being too shy to mention my dislike of snails – I got the wretched things down, somehow, but felt them crawling about in my stomach for several days. Now I love them!

Mark Cottenham, whose temperament was pretty restless, soon became bored with his mundane job and got himself transferred to a more interesting department. Jock Horsfall, too, was moved to another part of the Scrubs.

My next cell companion was an amusing young man called Charles Birkin – an old Etonian who, to the best of my knowledge, had never worked before. Not that he made a habit of indolence: I remember he helped me to brush up my spelling, in the intervals of treating the office as a place of high jinks.

Charles was the owner of a penthouse flat in Portman Square and I was sometimes invited to spend an evening there, in an atmosphere rather strikingly suggestive of pre-war calm and affluence – cook, valet and all. (My cell-mate was engaged to a beautiful young Australian actress called Janet Johnston who was just beginning to make a name for herself on the London stage.) Charles was famous for his parties and at one of these, when I was having an uproarious time with some Polish officers, my host's discreet 'Jeeves' tapped me on the shoulder and announced, 'Mr Birkin says he will take no responsibility for you if you dine with these gentlemen, miss.' This was a challenge, of course, so I left immediately, in the company of some high-spirited Poles, going on to the Bon Viveur in Shepherd Market, where the hilarity continued unabated, and getting home safely, in spite of Charles's misgivings.

I remember Charles on one occasion, when a rumour was

started to the effect that hot water was going to become unobtainable, calmly announcing that he intended to cut out washing! Unfortunately, he joined the army and his replacement was a rather pompous young barrister who pretty soon began to get me down. I disliked the way this newcomer blew his nose. I also found his heartiness too much to take at nine in the morning.

London was fun in the early part of the war, before the Blitz got under way (this was the period when more casualties occurred in the black-out, than as a result of enemy action); there was always someone to take you to a night-club like the Four Hundred or the Milroy, where you danced until the early hours. This meant you weren't always at your best first thing the following day. A short period for recuperation was needed – I asked nothing more than peace and quiet up until the coffee break at eleven, but my new cell-mate made sure I didn't get it. There are few things more dispiriting than sharing limited office accommodation with an uncongenial colleague; I began to dwell on the possibility of following Mark Cottenham's example and getting myself shifted out of 'A' Division.

'A' was the Division concerned with Administration; I fixed my sights on 'B' – Counter-espionage – which had a more colourful ring about it. There wasn't much I could do to effect a transfer, though; I simply kept my eyes and ears open and hoped to hear of something. I didn't overrate my abilities; I was taken by surprise when I was approached by 'B' Division – and not simply 'B', but a very select, clandestine sub-section within that division, B5(b).

It came about like this. One morning Bill Younger, whom I had often seen at the Scrubs and spoken to once or twice, came into my cell with a message from Maxwell Knight, the head of B5(b). I was invited to lunch in the staff canteen with this distinguished MI5 officer who, it seemed, had had his eye on me for some time. Naturally, I was intrigued and flattered. I knew Maxwell Knight by sight and reputation; I was aware that he ran B5(b) with no more than three or four case officers and a secretary, that he was known as 'M' or 'Max', that he cultivated some engaging eccentricities such as smoking long hand-made cigarettes from a little tobacconist's shop in Sloane Street. Rather tall and lanky, with a Wellingtonian nose which he referred to as 'my limb', always dressed in stylishly shabby tweeds, he made a conspicuous figure about the place. I was instantly aware of my good fortune and, at the same time, determined not to let it go to my head. I gratefully accepted the luncheon invitation, though.

At twelve-thirty I went into the canteen and saw Maxwell Knight at a table for two in the corner of the room. He got to his feet as I approached; even before he spoke, I was conscious of the charm this smiling man possessed – charm of a rare and formidable order. His voice, which I found hypnotic, confirmed the impression. By the end of that first lunchtime session I was capitvated. M, at the time, must have been about twice my age; it's possible, I suppose, that I had been subconsciously on the look-out for a 'father figure' – my own, an amiable, rather weak man who liked to gamble, hadn't exactly come up to scratch as a parent – but there was a great deal more than that to my feeling for M, even at this early stage.

Over lunch, I learnt a bit about his plans for me in the Division; and he suggested that we should dine together that evening, when he would go into the matter in greater detail. That gave me the afternoon to think it over. I wasn't in the least undecided, of course; I was ready to agree to anything put forward by M, and also tremendously excited by the prospect of getting to grips with work rather more exacting than anything I'd had to deal with in the transport office. I was already benefiting from M's ability to instil confidence and enthusiasm in his subordinates.

In the evening he took me to the Authors' Club in Whitehall Court. B5(b), he told me, over a protracted meal, was chiefly concerned with counter-subversion in this country, blocking the threat to British security from the Right as well as the Left (as Russia * was not yet in the war, the danger posed by the Comintern was very real). He mentioned the Right Club, of which I had barely heard, explaining that he wanted me to join this organization, passing myself off as an ardent Fascist, in order to keep a check on its activities. M already had two agents on the spot; one of these, an elderly lady known as 'Mrs Amos', had reported to him that the club was on the look-out for a recruit from the War Office. This was where I would come in.

I thought I could do it. First, however, it was necessary for me to understand as much as possible about Fascism in Britain, as well as the particular aims of extremist groups such as the Right Club; M would fill me in on the background, he said, and then it would be up to me. My course of instruction began the following day, when I started work in B5(b). Actually, the first thing I discovered was M's proper name: Charles Henry Maxwell Knight. (Most of his agents knew him as 'Captain King', though he was generally referred to as 'M' in the office. There is no doubt that the 'M' figure of the James Bond novels owes a great deal to Maxwell Knight, although this character is perhaps more closely modelled on John Godfrey, director of Naval Intelligence and a friend of Fleming's. Another Bond prototype may have been Gubbins of SOE, who also used the symbol 'M' and who was closer in appearance to the fictional 'M' than the large and burly Godfrey.) His closest associates at the time were Philip

* Russia, in fact, provided the Luftwaffe with the aviation fuel it used in the Battle of Britain and in the Blitz on London in the winter of 1940-41, and also supplied metal for German bomb cases.

Brocklehurst, a delightful man who was known as Brock; the famous detective novelist John Dickson Carr (John Dickson in the office); Guy Poston who, at forty or thereabouts, was too old to be called up; and the excellent Bill Younger, of the brewing family. Bill, slightly deformed from a childhood attack of polio, was a stepson of Dennis Wheatley and himself the author of some quite creditable poetry.

Bill had been an MI5 agent since his Oxford days, when M had recruited him to check up on some undergraduates propagating a rather noisy brand of pacificism in the wake of the celebrated motion passed at an Oxford Union debate that 'this House will in no circumstances fight for its King and Country'. M had become friendly with Dennis Wheatley, whom he met at one of Charles Birkin's parties in 1937; at this time, in the early part of the war, Wheatley's wife Joan, stepson and stepdaughter were also employed at the Scrubs.

These four – Bill Younger, Guy Poston, Brock and John Dickson – shared an office and ran agents under M's direction. M's expertise in this area was considerable; he had been involved in the business of infiltration since joining MI5 in 1924. In 1938, after eight years of exhaustive investigation on the part of Max and his team, a member of the Communist Party of Great Britain (CPGB) was brought to trial and convicted under the Official Secrets Act. This was Percy Glading, and the affair he directed came to be known as the Woolwich Arsenal case. While I was preparing to make bogus overtures to the founder members of the Right Club, Max got out the Woolwich Arsenal files – marked 'Closed Top Secret' – from their place in the Registry, and took me through the case, step by step. His idea was that I should learn how a really dedicated agent worked; and I was certainly impressed by the vigilance and perseverance shown by Olga Gray, who kept her wits about her through the whole dangerous course of the undertaking, and never lost credibility with the other side. She was only nineteen when Max persuaded her to take on the formidable job of obstructing a conspiracy to promote Communist interests in this country. Her first move was to join the Friends of the Soviet Union, and in a short time she managed to gain the confidence of Glading, who began entrusting her with delicate missions. Over the next seven years she was able to keep MI5 supplied with information about the activities of Britain's leading Soviet enthusiasts.

It's easy to see what made Max's department such a literary one; with so much dramatic material to hand, the impulse to make a high-class spy story out of it must have been pretty well irresistible to anyone with the least degree of narrative ability. The Woolwich Arsenal files were as full of intrigue as any work of fiction specially constructed to satisfy the avid thriller-reader: plots and plans, illicit photographs of naval guns, shifty foreigners, fateful attaché cases deposited in left-luggage compartments, conspicuous brown paper parcels passing from one impassive conspirator to another at Charing Cross Station. And, at the centre of it all, an MI5 agent keeping tabs on everyone around her and keeping her head at the same time. With the example of Olga Gray in front of me, and above all with Max's encouragement, I managed to ignore the perfectly reasonable qualms that assailed me whenever I envisaged myself in a similar role. Max easily convinced me of the value of the work; it was only my own competence I had doubts about.

The Right Club

THE RIGHT Club, which bore certain similarities to Admiral Sir Barry Domvile's organization, the Link, had been founded in 1938 by Captain Archibald Maule Ramsay, Unionist member for Peebles since 1931. Its members – about three hundred altogether, peers and MPs included – professed a belief in the ideal of an Anglo-German fellowship, as well as nurturing vigorous anti-Semitic feelings. Captain Ramsay was a friend of Sir Oswald Mosley. The Ramsays had a house in Onslow Square, but the club usually held its meetings in a flat above a little restaurant in South Kensington. This restaurant was the Russian Tea Rooms.

Early in 1940 M decided I was ready to go ahead with the task he had set me. I had already met Mrs Amos (Marjorie Mackie), one of the other agents involved in the business (a cosy middle-aged lady who will always remind me of Miss Marple), and it was arranged that she should take me along to the tea-shop one evening, presenting me as a friend of her son who was serving with the RNR. The restaurant was on the corner of Harrington Gardens, directly opposite South Kensington tube station. It was owned and run by an émigré White Russian admiral and his wife and daughter. These people, whose name was Wolkoff, had been dispossessed as a consequence of the Bolshevik revolution – Admiral Wolkoff had been the Tsar's naval attaché in London at the time – and understandably took a fervent anti-Communist line. Anna, the daughter, in particular, had come to revere the policies of Nazi Germany. From its inception, she had been among the leading activists of the Right Club.

It was a cold windy evening when I came out of the underground with Mrs Amos and crossed the road to the tea-rooms. The doors opened straight on to the street. Mrs Amos had described the old admiral to me, and, as we entered, I saw and recognized him at once: an upright, dignified, white-haired figure sitting aloof at a table, observing with detachment the comings and goings of his customers. He gave the impression of someone brought to a state of impassivity by the experience of countless vicissitudes.

The place was fairly crowded that evening, but we found an empty table, sat down and ordered tea. (You could actually get vodka here, long before it became a fashionable drink in this country, and also Russian foods like riaptchiki and caviar.) People around us were discussing the kinds of minor accident that occurred in the blackout, or lamenting in rueful voices the impossibility of obtaining certain necessities. These were among the standard topics of wartime conversation; you heard such unembittered complaints all over the place. Presently Anna Wolkoff came across the room, making her way through the polished tables, and stopped to speak to Mrs Amos who soon found an opportunity to bring me into the conversation, mentioning my supposed association with her son. Anna, who seemed prepared to be friendly in a guarded sort of way, asked what I did. I told her I worked at the War Office, laughed and added that really my job was a very boring one in a filing department. She nodded once or twice and passed on to something else. I could only hope I'd impressed her sufficiently to ensure that she remembered me when I next appeared.

The Russian Tea Rooms, with its polished wooden furniture, panelled walls and open fireplace, was the sort of café you could visit unescorted without jeopardizing your reputation. Over the next few weeks I made a habit of dropping in at all hours of the day, sometimes bringing along an innocent friend to lend colour to the deception I was engaged in. The old admiral used to join me quite often at my table where he would sit reminiscing about the past in Russia. 'No nonsense like these absurd licensing laws you have in England,' he would say, when his mood was jovial. I got to know Anna too, and whenever I spoke to her I put on a show of opposition to Britain's involvement in the war and support for the Fascist cause – not too emphatically at first, of course, but more openly as time went on. I invented a pre-war romance with a Nazi officer to account for these aberrant views. Anna, who was as wary and suspicious as a wildcat, listened to all this without giving anything away. When I insinuated that her experiences must have left her with strong opinions on these matters, she only smiled. I could sense that she approved of what I was saying, though. (I was learning!)

Anna Wolkoff had been born in Russia in 1902 or thereabouts, into a privileged family; and this made her the right age to suffer the fullest effects of enforced exile and impoverishment, with stories of Bolshevik atrocities to keep her

indignation active. After 1917 the Wolkoffs found themselves among the numerous other White Russian families
dispersed all over Europe. They were never in a frame of
mind to relish the colourful reversals of fortune that overtook
so many of their compatriots, refusing to have any truck with
a system that could allow a grand duke, for example, to wind
up as a gigolo or a waiter. Anna found as much solace as she
could in politics, becoming a right-wing agitator and crypto-
fascist. If it hadn't been for the war she might have gone on
in this way, unedifying as it was, without ever finding herself
in a position to do much damage. But in the peculiar conditions that prevailed in 1940, her pro-Nazi sympathies
acquired a very dangerous outlet.

She was short and dark-haired, not very impressive in
appearance, and displayed the intensity of manner which is
often associated with those of a fanatical disposition. She
took herself and her causes very seriously indeed. It was
difficult to get close to her as she was filled with mistrust, but,
once she'd accepted you, Anna was capable of impulsive and
generous acts. In spite of her upbringing she was a good cook
and this skill, I imagine, helped to keep the restaurant in
business; dressmaking, however, was her principal occupation (one of her clients was the Duchess of Windsor).
She owned the flat that served as headquarters for the Right
Club, as well as another one in Rowland Gardens.

One evening I was invited upstairs to eat one of Anna's
special omelettes with a small group of her friends. To reach
the flat you had to climb a narrow flight of stairs behind a
door in the tea-shop to the left of the entrance. I came up
these stairs with quaking knees. I was about to be vetted, I
knew, and if I failed to give a convincing performance I
would not only ruin the whole enterprise but also implicate
an agent greatly valued by M. I knew it was Mrs Amos's
testimony as much as anything else that had got me this far.
All this time she had been recommending me, with my War

Office connections, as a particularly useful recruit. At last it seemed the point had been taken.

Mrs Amos was among the group of ten or twelve assembled in the cramped sitting-room of Anna's flat, and so was Mrs Ramsay, wife of the misguided MP. I was introduced to her, and to a number of her friends. No men were present, partly because a lot of Right Club members had already been rounded up under Regulation 18b, and also because this was only an unofficial gathering. The women here were mostly senior club members and wives of internees. They were all considerably older than I was and regarded me, I thought, with a certain amount of curiosity.

'Joan has a great deal of common sense about political matters,' Mrs Amos said. 'She finds the War Office a bit of a bore.'

'Actually, I'm not too keen on war either,' I added. I didn't want to utter too many grotesque untruths, so I kept reiterating the same naïve illiberal sentiments, which went down well enough, as far as I could judge. I said the disaster for this country had been embarking on the war. I deplored the decision to jettison our policy of appeasement. I blamed the Government for its wrong-headed revulsion over Germany's imperialist ambitions. I complained about feeling cut off from the sense of being morally in the right that made things tolerable for everyone else. This elicited some sympathetic murmurs. Then, to my relief, the conversation became general and I was able to lapse into silence while I gathered my wits.

The next day M reported that I had passed the test: the ladies of the Right Club had taken my assertions at face value. Soon I was invited to join the organization: Mrs Ramsay put it to me that here was a way to help England. (These people all believed, sincerely I imagine, that they had the country's best interests at heart. Even the Wolkoffs weren't in the least anti-British; they simply associated the

Nazi movement with the possible liberation of Russia and supported it partly for this reason.) I assured her that nothing would please me more. 'I've felt so futile,' I said. A silver badge in a red case was found for me, and I began to attend meetings in the Harrington Gardens flat. (The badge depicted an eagle in the process of putting paid to a viper, the latter standing for the Communist and Jewish element in British society.)

How did these people set about obstructing the war effort? They used to sneak about late at night in the blackout, groping for smooth surfaces on which to paste the pro-German, anti-Semitic notices they carried. There were certain precautions one could take to lessen the likelihood of being arrested. Anna instructed her helpers to keep to the dark side of the road, paying particular attention to shadowy doorways where an alert policeman or air-raid warden might lurk, and to carry out the sticking while continuing to walk. These guidelines were issued to each member in the form of a printed sheet. Passersby who observed the Right Club's papers adhering to lamp posts, telephone kiosks, belisha beacons, church boards and so on, were informed that the war was a Jews' war. This was the Right Club's famous 'sticky-back' campaign. They also used greasepaint to deface ARP and casualty station posters. Jeering at Winston Churchill when he appeared on cinema newsreels was another of their practices. None of this could be said to constitute a serious threat to Londoners' morale; but there were, as it turned out, more sinister aspects to the organization.

By now I knew the identity of the third MI5 agent whom M had planted on the spot: this was Helen, a young, convent-educated Belgian girl. I'd seen her quite a few times at the Russian Tea Rooms, but for obvious reasons we had very little to do with one another. Helen, who had known Admiral Wolkoff since 1936, had also become friendly with Anna, on M's instructions.

Helen was in the habit of visiting relatives in Belgium, and Anna, knowing that she was about to make one such trip (this was in April 1940), gave her the task of consulting one of the Right Club's agents in Brussels about the trustworthiness of another. Anna presented her with a typewritten list of questions for the agent drafted in inferior French, which she was to learn by heart and then tear up. Helen proceeded to translate the document, which requested information about the progress of 'our work in Belgium', as well as containing encouraging news about the way things were going for the Right Club in England. She handed the translation to M, before leaving for Brussels where she dutifully performed all the tasks Anna had set her. On her return, a few days later, she was able to assure Anna that the agent she had doubted was completely loyal. She also passed on a message from her contact to the effect that Anna would do well to stop involving herself in such a devious and dangerous game. Probably Anna brushed this unwanted advice to one side; but undoubtedly she was very pleased with Helen's performance as an emissary.

M saw to it that I was kept in touch with these events. Through Mrs Amos, too, he had received information about the Right Club's plans for me. They hoped I might succeed in getting myself transferred to a department offering greater scope for sabotage. When Mrs Ramsay invited me to tea, I guessed the suggestion was about to be made. (The Ramsays' telephone line was tapped, but when the tape came through I learnt nothing of interest about the household, beyond the fact that the cook was helping herself to a good supply of sugar and butter.) It occurred to M that the machinations of this lady might be stopped once and for all if she were to make her seditious proposals in front of an audience. By this time my office had a good enough case to approach the Special Branch for their help. They agreed to co-operate; and it was decided that I should change the rendezvous to a

flat that could be wired and occupied by a couple of Special
Branch men in advance. I dialled the Onslow Square number.

'Mrs Ramsay? Joan Miller here. I'm sorry to change the
arrangement, but as it happens I've got to stay at home this
afternoon to take an important telephone call. Perhaps you
wouldn't mind joining me here for tea?' After a pause she
said that would suit her quite well; I gave her the address of
Philip Brocklehurst's flat in Pond Place which I had arranged
to borrow.

I collected the keys and dashed to the Fulham Road in
time to admit the two large Special Branch men who had
been detailed for the job. (As far as Mrs Ramsay was concerned, this was my day off.) They set to and wired the
sitting-room, before clearing a convenient cupboard and
arranging themselves inside it with a machine, ear-phones
and shorthand pads. We tested the system and found that,
with the window open, you could hear nothing but the traffic
in the Fulham Road. This was no good at all. The window
had to be kept closed however stifling the room became. It
was an exceptionally warm day, I remember. When my guest
arrived, wearing a hat, gloves, a dress and jacket, it was as if
she'd stepped into a greenhouse. 'Oh, my dear, can't we have
the window open?' she asked at once.

'I'm sorry,' I cried. 'The cat might jump on the window-sill
and fall into the street.' There was no cat, of course, but I
hoped she'd assume it was a timorous animal that kept well
away from strangers, and put my anxiety down to over-
protectiveness.

'Two inches?' she suggested. I told her the sashcords were
faulty, speaking with more vehemence than the occasion
required. She didn't persist, but sat pointedly fanning herself
with an old theatre programme someone had left on the
table. It wasn't a good beginning. I felt as inadequate as an
understudy unexpectedly thrust into the limelight on an
opening night – I knew the performance was doomed to

failure. What the policemen were going through in the cupboard I hardly dared imagine. It was up to me to direct the talk into productive channels, but all I could do was babble uselessly about the dreariness of my job and the awfulness of my employers. My prudent visitor didn't rise to the bait. 'I'm sorry you're unhappy in your work, Joan,' she said ironically.

I was actually quite relieved when she took herself off; nervous tension was making me overact to a dangerous degree. But how was I to placate two hot policemen whose time had been wasted? (In those days it was difficult to get the Special Branch to do this sort of thing.) They emerged from the cupboard mopping the sweat from their faces. Fortunately, after I'd given them some tea and made suitable apologies, they were ready to see the funny side of Mrs Ramsay's obstinate discretion. 'Not giving much away, was she?' they joked. 'You won't catch that old bird in a hurry.' I was grateful for their forbearance as well as being charmed by their jocularity, after all the quasi-Tuetonic intensity I'd been subjected to lately.

Next day I had to report to Brigadier 'Jasper' Harker, Deputy Director of MI5, who agreed I'd been unlucky and told me to try again. (He also sent me along to Special Branch Headquarters to apologize. They said, 'Don't worry, just give us a pin-up photograph of yourself' – so I did, and they kept it on the wall throughout the war.)

However, Mrs Ramsay soon repeated the invitation to Onslow Square and this time there was no getting out of it. Secure in her own drawing-room, she proceeded to incriminate herself as thoroughly as I could have wished – only of course there were no witnesses present. She leant forward, an intent look on her face, while pointing out how greatly the Right Club, and ultimately the country, might benefit from my initiative, if only I could arrange to have access to hush-hush material. I sat demurely on her sofa agreeing to fall in with these preposterous plans. I told her I would apply for a transfer right away, trying to seem flattered and excited by the trust she was placing in me. A few days later, acting on instructions from MI5, I sought out Mrs Ramsay to announce that my application had been successful; a spate of information, not very valuable at first and then more significant but out of date, quickly found its way, through me, to the Right Club's administrators.

As a result of this, my standing with this disreputable group was enhanced. Instead of merely building up a full list of Right Club members, as M had originally intended I should do (in conjunction with Mrs Amos), it was decided I might profitably devote my time to keeping tabs on Anna Wolkoff, who was now suspected of rather more than run-of-the-mill subversion. MI5 was in possession of evidence suggesting that some highly confidential communications between Churchill – then First Lord of the Admiralty – and Roosevelt had fallen into the hands of the German ambassador in Rome. It was of the utmost importance that these documents should have been kept secret; if it had been widely known, for example, that America enjoyed certain privileges with regard to shipping, other countries might have claimed similar concessions, with chaotic effects. A possible source of this disastrous leakage was the Italian Embassy in London, where an associate of Anna Wolkoff's was employed. But how had the carefully coded telegrams been deciphered? By this stage, everything pointed to a code and cipher clerk at the American Embassy – Tyler Kent, whose duty it was to transmit in code all telegrams handed on to him by his ambassador, Joseph Kennedy. Here was the culprit.

Tyler Kent had arrived in Britain in October 1939 after spending five years at the United States Embassy in Moscow. At this time, he appeared strongly anti-Communist and pro-Fascist in outlook.* As it turned out, he'd drawn atten-

---

* A *Times* article by the journalist and MI5 historian Nigel West,

tion to himself almost as soon as he got to London, by allowing a suspected Gestapo agent to visit him in his rooms. MI5 kept an eye on him from this point on, but took no immediate action. Kent actually made contact with the Russian Tea Room conspirators at the beginning of 1940, joining the Right Club shortly afterwards.

On the evidence of certain documents passing through his hands in the course of his work, Kent was strongly of the opinion that America's foreign policy had taken a disastrous turn. It was clear to him that Roosevelt planned to involve his country in the war, largely against the wishes of the American people. All documents tending to support this hypothesis, however obliquely, were copied by him and the copies transferred illegally from the embassy to his flat. It didn't take him long to amass a formidable collection. He intended to get this to the United States as soon as possible; once it became public property, he reasoned, it would furnish the isolationist movement with the power to defeat Roosevelt in the coming election. As far as Tyler Kent was concerned, the President was upholding America's neutrality in public, while actually planning to bring it to an end: such duplicity cried out for exposure.

It wasn't easy, however, to arrange for this top-secret material to be smuggled out of England; in the meantime, in

published in December 1983, suggests that Tyler Kent's activities were in fact undertaken on *behalf* of the Communists, and that his entire 'pro-Nazi' attitude was essentially a façade. According to Nigel West, the Tyler Kent case was reclassified after the war as pro-Communist motivated. Two things go to support his unorthodox view of Kent's behaviour: the Ribbentrop–Molotov pact, which remained in operation until June 1941, and made it possible to hold anti-Soviet and pro-Nazi sympathies simultaneously; and the fact that MI5's surveillance of the pro-Nazi faction at the time was in the hands of Anthony Blunt. However, I am not convinced that Kent was just as anti-Communist as he made out.

order to get the maximum advantage from having it in his possession, Kent suggested to his new friends, Anna Wolkoff and Captain Ramsay, that they might like to glance through it. They accepted his invitation with alacrity. This was in the spring of 1940. It is now generally agreed that Captain Ramsay was blameless as far as wishing for a German victory was concerned; he simply allowed his anti-Semitic obsession to get out of hand. His behaviour on this occasion, however, seems singularly incautious; what he did in effect was to sanction Kent's theft of diplomatic papers from the American Embassy.

What led Captain Ramsay to act in this extraordinary way? Kent, it appears, had offered to put him right about the causes of the war, a topic on which he said Ramsay was misinformed; perhaps the MP felt the benefit of having such crucial knowledge justified the breach of security involved in obtaining it. In the event, however, he showed more interest in the current conduct of the war than in its origins, paying particular attention to the Churchill/Roosevelt correspondence. The idea that he might raise a question in the House of Commons about whether or not Chamberlain was fully aware of his subordinate's growing association with the head of a foreign power, was mooted. He never got around to doing this.

Anna Wolkoff, who apparently had been struck by Captain Ramsay's interest in these particular documents, later returned on her own to ask Tyler Kent if she might borrow them. He, as he testified later, assumed she was acting on behalf of Captain Ramsay and blithely handed over the stolen papers. Anna took them off to a Russian photographer called Smirnoff, who was probably unaware of the importance of the documents and who quickly provided her with a number of prints. (These prints were never accounted for.)

By now, things were going badly for England. France had fallen; Mussolini had brought Italy into the war; the

Luftwaffe had established its supremacy in the air. As a consequence the Right Club was becoming increasingly incautious about expressing its views. With a German invasion expected at any moment, those who had all along supported Germany's claims believed themselves to be in a strong position. The society was engaged in compiling a list of prominent opponents to the Axis cause: if your name got on to this list you could expect to be strung up from a lamppost once the country was in German hands. I was consulted, I remember, over the question of who was to be classed as a fit candidate for lynching. I don't think I made any very sensible suggestion, but they kept pressing me to name the most vociferous anti-Nazis I had come across. They were adamant that an example must be made of these people to give the rest of the country a foretaste of the strong measures it could expect.

Throughout the spring and early summer, as far as I could manage it, I was keeping a close watch on Anna; this was a nerve-racking business as I half-expected her to pounce on me at any moment, with the remark that she knew exactly what I was up to. I continued to sense a certain watchfulness in her which I felt was directed at me. I had to keep reminding myself that I'd seriously wanted to be an actress – an ambition obstructed by my father's side of the family who had no wish to see any of my mother's characteristics reproduced in me – if I had any talent at all, I told myself, I should be able to play this part with conviction.

The situation was complicated, of course, by the fact that I felt no particular animosity towards Anna – if anything, I liked her – yet all my powers, at this moment, were concentrated on the effort to trap and disarm her. I fully understood the necessity for such action, it's true, and never for an instant doubted the wrong-headedness, and worse, of the position taken up by Anna and her associates. I knew quite well that they had to be stopped. Not only did the feeling in the Right Club run counter to the spirit of the country at large but there was something awfully squalid and painful in the clandestine goings-on initiated by Anna. There was, too, rather more than a hint of hysteria in her anti-Semitic outpourings. When her friends dubbed her – as a grim joke, I suppose – 'Julius Streicher', she didn't repudiate the nickname.

She could, however, as I've said, be extremely agreeable and even affable; in one of her moments of friendliness towards me she gave me a dress, a pre-war Worth in pink and blue, which was very smart. 'I have a present for you, Joan,' she said. I accepted it with very mixed feelings. Among M's basic rules for agents in my situation was one against vacill-ation which I found particularly useful. 'If you are going to tell a lie, tell a good one and above all stick to it,' he said. It wasn't my habit to lie and never has been, but for work on this case and others I found it paid to take a strong line at the beginning and never modify it, however much it was at odds with my genuine beliefs. After all, it was part of my job.

So, while Anna boasted to me about her contact at the Italian Embassy, and dropped hints about certain materials she intended to forward to the notorious traitor William Joyce (Lord Haw Haw), I tried to work out exactly how the information I was gathering could be used against her. An opportunity for action occurred quite fortuitously when her Italian friend, the Duke Del Monte, became ill; when she mentioned this fact to me, I told her (quite untruthfully) that I believed Helen was in a position to use the Romanian diplomatic bag. Anna lost no time in cornering Helen: 'Why didn't you tell me you had a friend at the Romanian Legation?' She went on to confess that she was in something of a quandary: she had in her possession a coded letter, addressed to William Joyce at the *Rundfunkhaus*, Berlin, and full of tips about the line he should take in his German propaganda broadcasts. Helen, briefed by M, offered to use her own contact to get this important missive on its way.

Once she got it into her hands, of course, she took it straight to M. The next morning, when she telephoned Anna to report that it had been duly dispatched, the volatile Russian lady didn't seem all that pleased. In fact she wondered if it might not be retrieved, for she now had something further to communicate to Joyce. Helen told her she would see what could be done. M, consulted once again, agreed that it would be helpful to have the postscript as well as the letter. Anna, when she was told that she might make the addition she wished ('You're in luck,' our agent said to her on the telephone), came round to Helen's flat to do so, and in fact typed her message to William Joyce on Helen's type-writer. She rounded off the letter with a drawing of an eagle and a snake – the Right Club emblem – and the letters P.J. – 'Perish Judah'.

Anna's letter, with these interesting additions, was re-turned to M, and he and I motored down to Bletchley, where the wartime decoding work was done. Twenty-four hours later the top boffins here, most of them pipe-smoking and donnish in appearance, it seemed to me, had failed to break the cipher. We were frantic. Then, suddenly, one of the boffins looked up and said, 'By God, this is an easy one. We've all been looking for something difficult.' We hurried back to London with the decoded letter (which, among other things, advised Joyce to stick to plutocracy in general and avoid making disparaging references to the King) and handed it over, with some deletions, to a contact of ours who really was in a position to use the Romanian bag (Mrs Amos's naval son, in fact, who was home on leave at the time). Lord Haw Haw duly acknowledged receipt of the letter, as he'd been instructed, by referring to Carlyle in one of his broadcasts.

MI5 was now ready to act. On 18 May, M approached the American ambassador, Joseph Kennedy, with a request that

Tyler Kent's diplomatic immunity should be waived. The request was granted, but the Americans were displeased to learn that, unknown to them, one of their employees had been under surveillance for some months. 'We should never have left the man in the code room if there had been the slightest ground for suspicion against him,' the Embassy's counsellor later wrote. (MI5's motives for keeping the Americans in the dark gave rise to a lot of speculation, at the time and afterwards; as far as I am aware, they were simply allowing Kent enough leeway to make the case against him watertight, and hoping that he would implicate others – as he did.)

On 20 May, M, accompanied by Detective Inspector Keeble, another officer and Franklin Crosbie Gowan of the American Embassy, led a raid on Tyler Kent's flat at 47 Gloucester Place. It was about eleven o'clock in the morning. When they banged on the door, Kent, who was in bed with his mistress, shouted out, 'You can't come in.' The raiding party wasted no time in arguing about the matter but simply forced an entrance. Once they'd broken into his flat the cipher clerk offered no further defiance. He stood and watched while M retrieved from a cupboard in his bed-sitting-room a brown leather portmanteau containing fifteen hundred stolen Embassy documents. These were all neatly sorted and filed. Kent was placed under arrest and taken to Cannon Row police station. Anna Wolkoff was picked up later on the same day, and both were held in custody until the autumn of that year, when they were tried separately, and *in camera*, at the Old Bailey. Captain Ramsay was arrested on 23 May and later interned, along with Sir Oswald Mosley. Many of their followers, respectively of the Right Club and the British Union of Fascists, were also taken up.

Helen's evidence, when she disclosed that all her activities, ostensibly on behalf of the Right Club, had in fact been monitored by MI5, helped to get Anna classified in court as a foreign agent, even though there was no suggestion that she had ever been in the *pay* of a foreign power, and thus affected the oucome of the Kent trial. Kent, known to have been associating with an enemy agent, was judged to have acted in a manner 'prejudicial to the interests of the state'. His trial took place first, in October, and he was found guilty, but not sentenced until the Wolkoff hearing had been completed. On 7 November 1940 the sentences were announced: seven years penal servitude for Tyler Kent, and ten for Anna.

I was obliged to give evidence at the Wolkoff trial, an ordeal I'd have found hard to endure if it hadn't been for M's constant support and encouragement. I remember standing beside him in the courtroom when Anna caught sight of me from the dock and started shouting abuse, among which I made out the threat to kill me, as soon as she was released. (In the event, she served her sentence, and died in a car crash shortly afterwards.) Certainly I understood that she had great cause for annoyance: three of her trusted associates having turned out to be members of the Security Service; on top of everything else, she must have felt this made her look pretty much of a fool. She tried to imply, in the course of giving evidence, that she'd suspected all of us all along, and indeed had engaged in various ploys to trap us; but none of this was exactly convincing. Her assertion, for instance, that her message for William Joyce referred to a meeting in Paris that never took place, and that she wrote it as part of a game of bluff she was playing with Helen, whom she suspected of being up to something, really made no sense.

However, I found the whole business pretty harrowing: the courtroom, the secrecy, the accusations, the inescapable sense of guilt over the part I had played in Anna's arrest. When the trial was over, I threw away the dress she had given me; I carefully cut off the buttons, though, and kept them in my 'memory' box.

B5(b)'s Country House

AT THE beginning of May, when the Wolkoff case was at its height, M sent me off one day to Camberley, in Surrey, to look for a house to rent. The one I eventually took was called 'Llanfoist'; set well back from the main London road, about a mile and a half outside Camberley, in grounds complete with stables and garages, and screened by a row of pine trees, it was ideal for our purposes. M needed the place as a retreat from the stresses of London, as a 'safe house' for agents, and as a spot where fellow MI5 officers, journalists and so forth, could be entertained overnight and work discussed.

Llanfoist, which belonged to an army officer posted abroad,

was let furnished. It must have been built about 1920, and contained nothing to distinguish it from any other large, unpicturesque, suburban family home of the period between the wars. Still, the rooms were spacious and pleasant enough, especially the drawing-room and the study which looked out on the garden; we had a gunroom too, as well as a conservatory built on to the front of the house, and enough bedrooms to put up guests. In these houses you always found a downstairs cloakroom exclusively for the chaps; ours was next to the dining-room on the ground floor. The household bathroom and w.c. were upstairs. Servants had their own quarters; and pretty miserable they were too.

What we required of the Camberley house was privacy and Llanfoist provided it. A brigadier's family named Caldwell lived near by, it's true, and we couldn't avoid getting to know them; however, they understood that our house was used for intelligence purposes and asked no questions. Whenever we stayed at Camberley, I acted as a hostess for M and ran the house with the help of a maid called Daisy. I don't think Daisy ever saw anything irregular in my position there; she knew that M was in the War Office and that I was his assistant, and that was enough for her. She was a simple-minded girl and, in common with many others of her background, she could only make sense of the war by envisaging it as something on a rather small scale. When reports of the evacuation from Dunkirk began to come through, I remember how hard we worked to keep Daisy in good spirits during the awful period of uncertainty while she waited for news of her husband. At last, as tired soldiers started to trickle back to their homes in Camberley, we learnt that he was safe. 'Well, of course,' Daisy announced at this point, with great pride, 'it was mostly Camberley boys at Dunkirk.'

In London, I still had my small basement flat in Anderson Street. When I moved from the Earl's Court hostel, shortly after joining Elizabeth Arden's, I'd taken two rooms at the top of a house off Coulson Street, also in Chelsea, but I left pretty quickly after coming face to face with a rat in the lavatory. The Anderson Street house was owned by a Norwegian actor; on the day when Norway was invaded I met him on the stairs, and the look on his face suggested he held me personally responsible for the disaster. He didn't speak; I thought he was going to spit. It was, of course, an emotional moment for him. Usually we were on the best of terms.

My closest friends at this period were a couple of young antiquarian booksellers called Peter Murray Hill and Peter Ducalion, who had a shop in Cecil Court, and Phyllis Calvert who later became a successful actress and film star. (They knew I worked at the War Office, of course, and also knew not to ask questions about my job.)

The two Peters had been my near neighbours in Anderson Street since before the war; but I'd been living there for some time before I actually met them. One day, a friend of mine at Elizabeth Arden's, an exuberant redhead called Eve Andrews, came to visit me. 'Isn't it dull!' she exclaimed. 'I know – let's have a party.'

'But who shall we ask?' I said. 'Why not wait until next week – Richard will be back soon.' (Richard Darwall, Eve's current boy friend, was staying in the country.) At this exact moment Eve happened to glance out of the window. 'Who are those two beautiful young men?' she asked. I urged her not to draw attention to herself, explaining that they were virtually my next-door neighbours, and that I'd never met them. But Eve wasn't to be restrained. The next minute she was leaning out of the window, her red hair stuck up on top of her head: 'Coo-ee!' she yelled. 'Come to a party?'

'Delighted!' they answered. So there we were. It was a sunny evening, a weekend, and nearly everyone we knew was out of London. 'You had better go and get some beer, or whatever,' I told Eve. 'This is all your doing – I wash my hands of it!' However, I did agree to telephone a few friends, and between us we managed to rope in enough people to make a reasonable crowd.

'You won't tell Richard what I've done, will you?' Eve said.

When the two Peters arrived I felt obliged to apologize to them. 'I don't do this sort of thing really – it's my friend!' I had reason to be grateful to Eve, though, as this was the start of a particularly high-spirited period in my life. I soon met Phyllis Calvert (who married Peter Murray Hill some time later), and a pattern was established whereby Phil and I took turns at cooking supper. (I was able to turn out a tolerable bread omelette, once Peter Ducalion had shown me how.) When we got tired of this, we would stroll round the corner to the Chelsea Pensioner in Lincoln Street, where the friendly owner and his wife allowed us to run up a bill. They were sweet: if they thought we looked particularly hungry, they would give us extra helpings, at no extra charge.

We were always running short of money, but for some reason this added to our constant state of hilarity more than anything else. It was an exhilarating time: for those who didn't have children or other relatives to worry about, London had a lot to offer – the stimulus of insecurity, I suppose, along with heightened awareness and the sense of being in the thick of things. War added an edge of vividness to every experience.

I had to rely on the two Peters to save me from starvation when a measles epidemic hit the Scrubs shortly after I started working there; I was among the last to catch the dread disease, but catch it I did, and I staggered back to Anderson Street one evening feeling considerably below par. What worried me most was the possibility of being packed off to some dreadful isolation ward in a hospital; for this reason I didn't want a doctor, and still less did I want my landlady to catch sight of the lurid spots which were coming up all over me. Three days was the maximum time I could take off work without a doctor's certificate; I hoped it would be enough. In the meantime, I needed something to eat. I managed to get one of the Peters on the telephone. 'Don't come near me,' I warned him, 'but *please* send round some food quickly. I'm starving.' I'd hoped for a very large loaf, or something of that sort, but I had to make do with some smoked salmon sandwiches which were lowered down to me at my basement window on a string.

Fortunately the spots went fairly quickly and I was able to return to the Scrubs. On my first morning back I was picked up by Jock Horsfall, who sometimes gave me a lift to work; I made him very angry indeed when I told him what had been the matter with me. 'How can you be so stupid and irresponsible?' I remember him shouting. I shouldn't have accepted his offer of a lift when I knew I was putting him at risk. I assured him I was better but he insisted I might still be infectious. It was important that he should not be put out of action. I think that was the first time I realized how crucial his role was; when something or someone needed to be taken to a particular location at top speed, it was usually Jock who got the job. He was fast, and not often reckless – though I remember Mark Cottenham reprimanding him on one occasion for the foolhardy way he skidded round Hyde Park Corner: 'You, as a racing driver, jolly well ought to know better,' Mark told him. One of our most colourful agents, Dusko Popov (one of Fleming's models for the character of James Bond), was met by Jock at Felton Airport when he first arrived in England. Unfortunately, Jock Horsfall became our first casualty at the Scrubs; towards the end of 1940, when he was on fire-watching duty, an incendiary bomb landed on 'C' wing and he fell through the roof while fighting the blaze, injuring his neck quite badly.

A lot of informal social activity went on in the evenings at my Anderson Street flat, with people of my own age cons-

tantly dropping in. I found this very relaxing; I was happy to
forget my work in the transport section of MI5 until the
alarm went off at seven-thirty in the morning. As soon as I
joined B5(b), however, M started to affect my life in all sorts
of ways. He made it clear to me, and to everyone else, that I
was in a special position as far as he was concerned. His
colleague Philip Brocklehurst actually became rather alarmed
on my behalf, and took me out to lunch one day for the sole
purpose of disclosing that M, in fact, had a wife. I must say I
didn't find this information in the least disquieting. I had
hardly expected otherwise – and besides, I was sufficiently
captivated by this time to be pleased with M's friendship, on
any terms he cared to offer.

M was enigmatic and debonair, qualities I found irresistible, as well as being deeply knowledgeable on a wide variety
of subjects. This made him a fascinating companion. The
range of his accomplishments was extraordinary. He'd played
the drums in a jazz band at the Hammersmith Palais; and,
more impressively, he was equally proficient on the clarinet.
He might have made a living as a schoolmaster if he hadn't
found that profession unendurably tame. For a short period
he ran a small hotel on Exmoor with his first wife Gladys, at
the same time working as a riding instructor. (It was during
this time – according to a rumour – that M was suspected of
being a werewolf!). He published a couple of thrillers before
the war, *Crime Cargo* (1934) and *Gunmen's Holiday* (1935),
both of which I read with some enjoyment though he himself
had a low opinion of them. He was a Fellow of the Royal
Zoological Society and a keen naturalist. He knew more
about the occult than anyone I've ever met, including Dennis
Wheatley. (Like Wheatley, though a few years later, he'd
spent some time as a naval cadet on the training ship
Worcester.) He was a crack shot, and also a collector of
antique guns. Botany, ornithology and literature were among
his enthusiasms. I didn't acquire all this information at once,

of course – M was never very forthcoming about his own affairs. I think it pleased him to display an air of secrecy; certainly he discouraged questions about the past. The 'Captain King' role, dangerous and mysterious, suited him down to the ground. He wore his affectations lightly, though; among his assets was a sense of humour, without which he'd hardly have made such a success of running B5(b).

He never told me much about his parents or his childhood, as far as I can remember, and it wouldn't have occurred to me to cross-question him; I've always found the desire for privacy a perfectly reasonable one. Besides, at that time, one lived in the present; the past was unimportant and the future chancy. I couldn't help picking up bits and pieces, though, from M himself and from others associated with him. I know he was born at South Norwood, in south-east London, that his father was a solicitor and that his mother had been married before. But these prosaic facts give no clue at all to M's distinctive personality.

There are others which are more telling, though still obscure. His first wife Gladys, I learnt, died in the Overseas Club after some sort of occult misadventure in which the notorious Aleister Crowley was involved – certainly I'd have been unwilling to enquire too deeply into that particular incident. Black magic was not a subject that held any attraction for me. I accepted M's interest in it, hoping it was purely academic, but, for myself, I preferred to leave it well and truly alone: M understood this. When I tore up a photograph of Aleister Crowley which he had kept, as I believed it to be unlucky, he only laughed.

When I first met him, M was married to Lois Coplestone and lived with her in a flat above a shop in Sloane Street, (where, for a time, he kept a bush baby as a pet, as well as other animals). Soon afterwards he moved to a one-room bachelor flat in Dolphin Square (608 Hood House), which had belonged to his brother-in-law, the late Anthony

Coplestone. Much later, I came to know M's elder, unmarried sister Enid by sight – she went in for good works, I think, holding some sort of voluntary post at Chelsea Town Hall – but I never met her; naturally she would have disapproved of me.

In the spring and summer of 1940 my education was taken in hand by M. We used to visit the London Zoo on Sundays, for example – he as a Fellow of the RZS had free access, though it was closed to the public on that day of the week – where the habits and peculiarities of various animals were described to me. M knew the correct method of mounting a llama as well as being thoroughly familiar with the breeding cycle of the laughing hyena. I absorbed as much information as I could. I drew the line at the Reptile House, however, as I am afflicted with that very common phobia, a fear of snakes. From his splendid Cockney daily Mrs Leather I'd gathered that M had kept some snakes in his flat, before the war put a stop to this particular eccentricity. ('They used to flop down the stairs,' she said. 'Mr Knight – he was a one!') I assured him he had only to repeat the exercise if he wanted to see the last of me. (Once, I learnt to my horror, he had raised a nest of adder eggs in his pyjama pocket).

The zoo visits were alternated with days in the country in the course of which I added plant-identification and the recognition of certain bird calls to my new store of knowledge. All this was highly enjoyable, and very gratifying for me, especially as I'd never received this sort of productive attention from either of my parents. What I found most overwhelming, though, was the way M used to send taxi-loads of presents round to my flat – enormous bunches of flowers, mostly, and bowls arranged by Moyses Stevens as well as books and so forth. 'That man' was the way he signed himself; all these were accompanied by a note which ended, 'With that man's love'. He went to endless lengths to keep me amused and happy; one day, for example, an 'old time blues song', composed by M, arrived in the post. 'Mean Joan', it was called.

> Way out west where the grass is green,
> Little Miss Joan she's a poison queen.
> If you treat her bad she'll treat you mean
> She's the meanest dame you've ever seen.
>
> She's easy on the eye but quick on the draw,
> She don't give a damn for old man Law.
> Her heart's as tough as a graveyard stone,
> She's death in skirts is Little Miss Joan.
>
> 'That man' came along with a six-shot gun,
> Said he, 'I'm goin' to have some fun.'
> He took out a dime and reached for the phone
> And put through a call to lil' Miss Joan.
>
> . . . In Luke's Saloon this tough dame sat,
> Fingering gently her favourite 'gat'.
> The big swing door flapped open wide,
> An' that man swaggered himself inside.
>
> He looked around and he gave a smile,
> When he saw Mean Joan he paused a while.
> Then he crossed to the bar an' winked his eye,
> And cried, 'Set 'em up for Miss Joan and I.'

The upshot of all this is that she puts a bullet through him, 'For she likes 'em better dead does Mean Miss Joan'. Who could resist such a singular love song?

One day I was standing in the hall with an armful of spring flowers, which a lugubrious taxi-driver had just deposited on my doorstep, when my old friend Peter Ducalion, home on leave, came wandering in. (He had joined the Cavalry in the autumn of 1934.) He took in the scene at a glance, crossed the living-room and removed from the wall a picture he'd lent me, a sketch of himself by August John. 'I think I had better relieve you of this,' he said. There was no animosity in his action; he was just letting me know that he understood the score. I didn't say a word, or raise a finger to stop him as he walked out. What could I do?

It was about this time that M acquired a second flat in Dolphin Square, No. 10 Collingwood House, and suggested to me, in a letter, that I should take it over. 'You see, I really need to have you close,' he wrote. 'Otherwise I don't think I can carry on with this nerve-straining work. You take my mind off things.' It was an appeal, and I answered it. I remember offering to furnish the place myself – a last gesture of independence – and M agreed.

In those days the Dolphin Square complex, built by an up-and-coming young architect called Richard Costain, was *the* most modern concrete high-rise structure in London. Each block of flats consisted of seven storeys, I think, with shops, restaurant and swimming-pool included in the overall plan. Maid service was provided, and we had our own taxi firm on the spot. No. 10 Collingwood House was a two-room, ground-floor flat overlooking the 'drive-in'. It contained a windowless hall where I remember dragging a mattress once or twice whenever the air-raids had started in earnest – there were very adequate shelters underneath each building but I detested the thought of being cooped up in one with a lot of apprehensive strangers. The risk seemed trivial compared with the prospect of enduring such discomfort.

'You must tell everyone you've left London for a time in connection with your job,' M announced one day. I agreed there was some sense in this as I was by now working very closely with M and really didn't want outside distractions; the old Anderson Street life no longer seemed as satisfactory as it had a short time earlier. In this way M succeeded in cutting me off from all my friends who, I think, imagined me engaged in secret work in some bleak inaccessible compound in the heart of the country, while all the time I was living in comfort in Dolphin Square.

One of my new neighbours was Arthur Greenwood, a minister in the coalition government, whom I used to see occasionally in the Dolphin Square restaurant. Once, I remember, he beckoned to me: 'I want to talk to you.' At the time, if you got a taxi at all, it dropped you at Victoria, and you walked the rest of the way to Dolphin Square. Bagsnatching had suddenly become common in the area, and Arthur Greenwood – a very kind man – was worried that I might be subject to some such attack. 'You won't know how to deal with it,' he said. 'Let me show you.' He taught me a trick from his Gorbals boyhood. 'Put pennies between your fingers – like this – and hit *hard.*' I was very grateful for his advice, though I never actually needed to put it into practice!

All in all, I was fairly well protected. Among M's more exotic presents to me were a leather-covered cosh from Tom Hill in Knightsbridge, and a small gun – a sort of stocking gun really, but none the less lethal for that. After the Wolkoff case I was on various black lists, I suppose, and therefore better armed in case of invasion. When I look back to that period I sometimes get an image of myself, in the garden at Camberley, in well-worn ski trousers, gumboots and an old hacking jacket of my mother's, blazing away at a target set up by M; or, more innocently, learning the techniques of fly-fishing with the aid of a pudding basin on the lawn. M made me keep at things until I got them right. I see M too, one of his special cigarettes perpetually in his mouth, stretched in an armchair in a rare moment of relaxation with a copy of Damon Runyon's stories by his side, or crawling on hands and knees in pursuit of some unlikely insect or animal. (Small wonder that the title of one of the books he published after the war was *Hints to Young Naturalists.*) I remember him too, suddenly immobilized by a plan of action which came into his head, standing with a pair of drumsticks in his hand while he worked out the details; or beating out a tune on the marble mantelpiece at Camberley – Jimmy Noon's 'Sand', most likely, 'Nobody's Sweetheart', 'Saratoga Swing', or 'Dixieland'. These pieces were all popular at the time, and M certainly enjoyed them as much as anyone.

It's an idyllic picture, of course. Certainly we had moments of friction and distress, though it wasn't until much later that these became at all persistent. In the beginning I accepted everything I was told and never looked for flaws in the eventful life I was leading. The office kept us all continuously on the alert and left us with little time to dwell on our own concerns. Of course, the atmosphere was especially conducive to the forming of brief passionate attachments and the flaring up of sudden uncontrollable feelings. The air around us was thick with anticipations, many of which were realized.

Once Anna Wolkoff was placed under arrest, my cover was blown as far as the extreme Right was concerned. There was still plenty for me to do, however. The Communist Party Headquarters at King Street, Covent Garden, was well covered by MI5 with agents posing as Soviet supporters and effective telephone interception. (Tom Driberg, whom M had recruited before the war, was active here until his identity was discovered by Anthony Blunt, who passed on his information to the Russians, causing Driberg to be expelled from the Party.) One call, intercepted by us, directed our attention to a deed box hidden under the bed of Rajani Palme Dutt, a well-known lawyer and CP member, whose name was often found attached to articles in extreme left-wing journals such as the *Labour Monthly*.

The task of investigating this box and its contents was allocated to me. First, I was sent off to a very special department of the Post Office and here, under instruction, I quickly became adept at opening and resealing letters; there was no place in the office for shilly-shally or amateur bungling. The mechanics of breaking open a locked trunk were then disclosed to me. Equipped with these skills, I was in a position to get to the bottom of the deed box. Breaking and entering *toute seule* didn't exactly appeal to me, however. Guy Poston came to the rescue. 'We'll do it together,' he said.

Knowing the Dutts were away from home, we made an unlawful entry into their terraced house not far from the Scrubs. Guy picked the Yale lock while I stood uneasily beside him, expecting all the while to be challenged by an outraged neighbour. However, we broke in safely and wasted no time in getting up the stairs and scrabbling about under the matrimonial bed for the locked box, which we found easily enough, rather to my surprise. Sitting on the linoleum-covered floor of Palme Dutt's bedroom, I opened first the box and then the sealed envelope I found inside it, in the way I'd been taught. We eagerly pored over this important document – and then burst out laughing. 'All this trouble, and what do we get?' Guy groaned. 'A copy of the poor chap's marriage lines.' Back into the box it went, while we exchanged rueful glances; a cursory search of the house didn't reveal anything incriminating either, so we took ourselves back to the Scrubs feeling slightly abashed. It didn't help when M persisted in treating the episode as a joke.

It *was* amusing, of course, in the way it turned out; but all the time I was in that house I had to fight hard to overcome an instinctive aversion to tampering with other people's belongings; this was an aspect of security work I never enjoyed. It was even worse when I knew the person concerned — which happened once or twice. The instance of unwelcome searching I remember most clearly is the one connected with the Krishna Menon affair.

Krishna Menon, at the time, was a borough councillor for St Pancras, as well as being an Indian nationalist and left-wing agitator whose views seemed sufficiently extreme to mark him off as a potential danger to British security.* He was picked out for close investigation, and the job was given to me. I went along to one or two of his political meetings and met him afterwards, with the result that I asked to be taken off the case. 'I'm sorry,' I told M, 'I can't be of any help to you here at all.' It was plain to me that the man was unhinged on the subject of the British and the way they'd mishandled affairs in India; at the root of all this was a personal grievance on account of his father, a small-time civil servant in Kerala who'd been badly done by. I never learnt the true facts of his history; the way Krishna Menon ranted against the Empire was enough to discourage me from involving myself any further in the business. Not that I was Empire-minded, particularly; it was simply a clash of temperaments. There was nothing I could do to get through to this man.

Helen, the third of M's Right Club infiltrators and one of his most useful agents, was then put on to the case. She was an excellent choice, being the sort of girl who could creep into a red-hot political meeting and remain unnoticed, but also someone who never failed to make a good impression when she wanted to. With Krishna Menon, she didn't have to overcome the initial disadvantage of being English. A convent background and moderate attractiveness added to the trustworthy effect she created. She handled the job very efficiently, feeding us with relevant information and keeping Krishna Menon satisfied at the same time. Unfortunately he fell in love with her and this led to a number of complications. Helen, unknown to us, was in the throes of a reckless affair with her case officer; stress, perhaps caused by Krishna

* He later became High Commissioner for India, ambassador to the Republic of Ireland, and first editor of Pelican Books; he died in 1974.

Menon's attentions on top of this, made her give in to a craving she'd indulged before: drugs.

One morning she was due at the office with an important report and failed to turn up. Her case officer, who, at this point, should have made the necessary investigations, wasn't available either. So it fell to me to track her down. She was living in a small flat of ours in Chelsea and I was able to visit her there without jeopardizing her cover or my own, because the circles we moved in were usually completely different. (The Wolkoff case excepted; Krishna Menon had only been a flash in the pan as far as I was concerned.) I rang to let her know I was on my way, but got no reply. This worried me slightly, so I pocketed the duplicate key to her flat which was kept in the office safe.

I found Helen in bed in a state of delirium – the sight shocked me as it was the first time I'd observed the effect of drugs. In fact I hardly knew what was wrong with her until I got through on the phone to M who put me straight. He then instructed me to search the room while I waited for the office doctor to arrive. 'Turn it inside out,' he said. It required an effort to suppress my repugnance at the whole business. No drugs and no correspondence from Krishna Menon came to light, but I uncovered hundreds of love letters to Helen from her case officer, a married man well known to M and me – I couldn't condone such reprehensible and foolhardy behaviour. Anyone could tell that Helen, with her history of drug-taking, was an insecure girl who shouldn't be subject to this kind of pressure. I was so cross with the man that I gathered the letters into a bundle, carried them back to the office and dumped them on M's desk.

Of course, it would have been more tactful to return the letters to the case officer concerned; I'd have done this in different circumstances but it was out of the question when a possible security risk was indicated. I knew I wasn't going to be popular in the office for a time – I felt rather like the sneak of the fourth form in a pre-war school story. 'Please take it gently,' I said to M. In fact, he had every intention of doing so – not to save my face so much as his own. It was important that no rumours of promiscuity should reach the top men in our headquarters. Such goings-on were considered *the* number one security risk – and M, of course, was responsible for what went on in his section. I remember him once remarking that you could get away with leaving vital documents on a bus, or any other sort of carelessness – but heaven help you if you were caught with your secretary on your knee. So M covered up, to an extent, for Helen's lover, warning him, however, that his wife would be told if the affair continued. Helen had treatment for drug-addiction at a very private clinic and eventually recovered sufficiently to resume working for us under different management. (I saw Helen just once after that morning when she lay groaning and raving on the bed, in the summer of 1951, walking down the Rue d'Antibes in Cannes. As she was accompanied by two children I deduced she had got a job as an au pair. I let her pass without speaking; the war was far behind me, and I had no wish, just then, to be reminded of the strains and tensions of those years. Now I am sorry I didn't stop her; though I never knew her well I liked Helen, and always thought of her as a first-class agent.)

There were, of course, certain ironies in the position taken up by M, in view of his relationship with me. He'd virtually moved in to my Dolphin Square flat, and it was accepted by everyone that I was his mistress. There were reasons for M's comparative openness about this matter which I didn't understand at the time. When the bombing of London started his wife Lois was evacuated to the country, becoming secretary to the Chief Constable of Oxfordshire, Eric St Johnston (a friend of the Knights since 1937), and working at Police Headquarters there for the next few years. The couple had separated before this, of course, though they remained on friendly terms; M quite often travelled down to Oxford to stay with Lois at the St Johnstons' house.

I had no objection to being taken for M's mistress although, in fact, the situation was by no means simple. The fact that our affair remained unconsummated I put down to my own inexperience of these matters – I was only twenty-two, and I'd led the usual tame, decorous life of a well-brought-up girl before joining MI5 – combined with the effects of some traumatic incident in M's past – connected with his second wife, I believed. It was very difficult to associate M with incapacity in any area. I was assured that the problem was temporary, and largely created by me and my incompetence, and I was grateful to M for not making more of a fuss about it. He kept telling me not to worry, that it would be all right in the end.

The early incendiary bomb which caused the injury to Jock Horsfall also damaged the Registry at the Scrubs* and shortly after this came the announcement that MI5 would now be housed elsewhere. The main office was transferred to a large new block in St James's Street, originally taken by MGM, I think, but never used because of the war. Most of the subsidiary departments were moved to Blenheim Palace, one wing being reserved for the Duke and his family while the office occupied the rest of the building. The Duke was very long-suffering over the inconvenience caused to him, and the unsightliness of the Nisson huts which pretty soon began to clutter the estate. Still, I think he derived a lot of enjoyment from the presence of all the pretty blondes whom MI5 employed in one capacity or another – it was always blondes, I remember, and the favourites changed from month to month with no harm done and a good deal of pleasure had by all. Members of the 'firm' were billeted out, usually in the

* This fire at the Scrubs was rumoured to have destroyed quite a number of MI5 files of considerable importance.

sort of large, imposing old house which cold makes virtually uninhabitable in winter. The War Office requisitioned Keble College too; this was strictly girls' quarters. The old scouts remained and made themselves very agreeable to us, but the place was draughty and uncomfortable. I used to stay at Keble whenever I was required to put in a day's work at Blenheim. One night I lay there, unable to sleep, listening with dismay to the throb of German planes passing overhead, considering the location of Oxford on the map of England, and imagining the horrors of bombing inflicted on civilians somewhere to the west: it was, in fact, the night of the first Coventry raid.

B5(b), at M's insistence, was kept separate from the main office after the move from the Scrubs and installed, by a piece of luck, in a further flat in Dolphin Square annexed by M. This one was a ground-floor flat, in a block situated to the right of Collingwood, and large enough to suit our purposes. M's idea was to establish a perfectly secret division here – but in fact our existence was known to the Abwehr as early as 1941. No one took into account, either, the fact that we were very close to the Battersea power stations which were a continual target for the Luftwaffe, though, as it happened, the Germans never succeeded in paralysing both at once. We never got used to the noise of enemy planes droning overhead, and the constant fire-fighting, clearing-up activity and rescue operations going on all around made it difficult, too, to concentrate on what you were doing. There were two direct hits on Dolphin Squre while I lived there; one bomb (about 500 lbs was the standard weight in those days) went through the top two floors of Frobisher House, and the other fell at an oblique angle, demolishing part of an underground shelter and killing or injuring a number of those taking refuge there.

I remember with outstanding clarity the first raids which occurred on a hot September afternoon in 1940. I was at home answering a letter from my old headmistress who'd written to ask for news of my activities for the school magazine. I was, in fact, the third old girl* who'd ended up in MI5 (not a bad record for a school with only sixty-five pupils); but of course, for security reasons, I had to fall back on the old euphemism about working at the War Office. I wondered how she'd react if I were to describe in detail the exigencies of my job, mentioning also the ways in which I was and was not my boss's mistress. Actually, I am sure she would have understood; she always did. I was just in the act of composing a bland little paragraph full of chatty, personal observations, when the first crunch came out of the bright sunshine. It was very near. I stopped writing, and somehow the letter never got finished.

By the evening the East End of London was ablaze. From the roof of Collingwood, with M by my side, I watched the docks burning. The sky, in which white vapour trails from warring aircraft were a common sight, was lit with an unearthly glow. The heat and the smoke were appalling. Before morning, a thousand Londoners would have died in this unspeakable attack. I was overtaken by a sense of rage and helplessness; later, I trained myself to stop thinking about the sufferings of victims – if you dwelt on the horrors it became impossible to carry on. The indispensible quality at

---

* One of the others was Janet Withers, who got me into MI5 in the first place: she was always my close friend, ever since the days when she took me under her wing at boarding-school (she was two years older), and showed me how to make my bed and do up my shoelaces. When the Registry moved to Blenheim, I used to lunch with her there quite frequently. She became rather agrieved, though, by the fact that I continued to prosper, in a way, at MI5, while she remained stuck where she'd started. 'I really can't understand why *you* should have got on so well!' she would say. 'Why haven't I?' Janet stayed with MI5 until she retired a few years ago, shortly before her death.

that period was resilience; you were required to show your stamina all the time. There was no question of giving way to inexpedient emotions. I suppressed my abhorrence for what was taking place around me and this feeling did not reassert itself until the occasion when, years later, I went to see a war film and had to leave the cinema because I could not bear the sound of bombs going off. In 1940, the Blitz was merely inconvenient and tiresome, interfering with work and keeping you awake half the night. On M's advice, I began taking pills to sleep through the infernal noise, and, as a consequence, I've suffered from insomnia ever since.

'The Camberley
Menagerie'

W E WERE all jubilant over the new office arrangements. M and I shared the largest room, working
at desks which faced one another with a good
distance in between. Paper-work held no appeal at all for M,
so most of this fell to my lot. *He* seemed to be under the
impression that things left in the in-tray would eventually
sort themselves out by some mysterious process not involving
his co-operation. I did as much as I could to make things easy
for him. I didn't mind this, though some of it was extremely
boring, because I felt I was learning all the time.

A door in this main office led into a smaller room where
our zany telephonist-cum-filing-clerk, Babe Holt, was in-

stalled. Both Babe and I came from the West Country, and I'd known her slightly before the war, when we used to bump into one another at hunt-balls and other social occasions. She was a real blonde, very decorative to look at and great fun, though highly disorganized; the office switchboard, with Babe in charge of it, did not function in the way it should have. Certainly she was not employed on account of her efficiency. Like the rest of us girls, though, she was absolutely trustworthy and discreet, as well as adding considerably to the gaiety of things.

M's new secretary was a nice quiet girl called Liz Seale who suspected us all of being somewhat mad. We had gained some new associates since leaving the Scrubs, and lost others: Guy Poston had left, as well as John Dickson Carr; Brock had rejoined his old regiment (he was later drowned in Burma); and the B5(b) secretary Felicity Reid had gone on to work for Tar Robertson of BI(a) (specializing in counter-espionage against Germany). Bill Younger was still with us, fortunately, and we had acquired a journalist as well as a fiery little red-headed newspaper reporter from the Midlands.

There were also quite a few part-time members of staff (usually waiting to be called up, or just on the brink of being over the required age), like Tony Gilson, a glamorous young man with a flat in Grosvenor Square and a well-known place in the Cotswolds with the rather confusing name of Cornwall, who, for a time, kept the upper reaches of café society well covered on our behalf. (It was remarkable how high-ranking officers liked to boast, and how indiscreet some of them were capable of being.) Tony's services were invaluable to us – our petty-cash box certainly wouldn't have run to innumerable evenings out at the Four Hundred, the Berkeley, the Savoy and other places of this sort, which he frequented as a matter of course, coming away, in the early hours of the morning, with many useful small pieces of intelligence information. With his wife and child evacuated to America, Tony felt free to fall in love, which he did whole-heartedly, though not happily. Rose Bingham – as she was before her marriages, in succession, to the Earl of Warwick and an American fighter pilot named Billy Fiske – one of the last of the great debs, beautiful and self-possessed, gave him so little encouragement that he joined SOE in an excess of frustration. He was immediately sent on a mission to India, and the aeroplane in which he was travelling was blown off course and never heard of again. I imagine it went down in the Indian Ocean where the crew and passengers died, one hoped, before the sharks got them.

As well as dealing with the paper-work, and continually checking things to ensure that the office was running smoothly, I was landed with the dreariest job of all: looking into the innumerable reports from people who dutifully communicated to the authorities their suspicions of some harmless character they took to be a Fifth Columnist. Spy-fever was upon us. When I first joined the office John Dickson Carr had warned me against falling into the state of mind where you saw spies round every corner – an occupational hazard for people in our position, he said. I never did get into this state, but I observed it constantly in members of the public who subscribed all too thoroughly to the doctrine of incessant vigilance urged on them from above. Nigel West, in his book on MI5, has a story about a new recruit immediately sent out to inspect every telegraph pole in the southern counties and draft a security report on each. A claim had reached the War Office that coded messages had been left on these poles for the benefit of enemy parachutists.

This is the sort of thing we were up against all the time: every report had to be investigated, even the most lunatic, with the exception of those concerning telephone tapping, over which the Home Office, quite rightly, took a firm stand. Reports of tampering with a telepone line were simply too numerous and insubstantial to be worth the bother of checking, unless there was some factor which made the case seem really urgent. Being the only woman officer in my department ('acting civil servant' was the official title), I was frequently obliged to visit, and calm down, some dotty old lady in a state of fright. These old ladies were for ever glimpsing spies under their beds, or finding themselves trailed by one, for some sinister purpose, on the way home from an outing.

What passed for patriotic behaviour was all too often grounded on an instinct for self-dramatization. Most of the reports we received were, in fact, perfectly sincere, if ill-founded; but occasionally one would arrive from some neur-otic individual who hardly knew how to distinguish between truth and fantasy. I remember the first time I went with M to cross-examine one of these sensation-seekers. We'd been working hard all morning, and it was already one o'clock when M turned to me and asked if I was ready for lunch. I nodded. 'Good,' he said. 'I've booked a table at Hatchetts.' It struck me that this was a rather unlikely setting for such a routine interview as I expected. 'Of course, if anything really interesting should come up,' M said, poker-faced, 'we can move on to Room 005 after lunch.' (This was the official interviewing room.) 'Just remember, Joan, to keep quiet and let me do the talking.'

The girl in question, an ATS worker at a coastal service telephone exchange, had been sent to us by the War Office proper, where her allegation had made some impression. She'd come up with some astonishing information concerning listening devices, secret lines and mysterious voices coming through on the telephone. The latter, she claimed, had made her very nervous by insisting that 'They' had marked her out for some key collaborationist position after the invasion.

It was M's practice to be late for an appointment when he wished to gain a slight psychological advantage. The ATS girl was waiting when we arrived at Hatchetts. She was very plain, having lank hair the colour of margarine, and skin to match, poor soul. We sat down and M ordered drinks, followed by smoked salmon. The entire story of the jinxed telephone lines was repeated for our benefit. I must confess I found it interesting and plausible. You would have thought M did too, as he subjected the girl to close questioning, nodding at appropriate moments and never taking his eyes off her pasty face. After the smoked salmon, however, he suddenly remarked, 'Dear me, you *are* a silly girl. You know none of this is true, so now please take yourself back to your unit and let's have no more nonsense.'

A look of consternation came over her face; she got up abruptly, nearly knocking her chair over, and burst into tears. M sat calmly on. I hurried her off to the ladies' room, mopped her up and sent her on her way, still sniffling. When I got back to our table M was ordering the next course. 'Are you sure you haven't made a ghastly mistake?' I asked.

'My dear Joan,' M replied. 'Let's just take it step by step.' So we went over the whole business again, and this time I saw the inconsistency in the elaborate story which M's years of listening and watching had enabled him to spot at once. 'Oh, gosh,' I said. It wasn't an adequate comment but it was all I could manage. I returned to the office greatly impressed by M's tactics as an interrogator.

I had one particular asset at this time as far as M's outside work was concerned – a good memory. I was able to sit in at an interview, listen to what was being said, and then, back at my desk, put down on paper the entire conversation – all without taking notes on the spot, which might have had a distracting effect on the other person. I wrote these resumés in pencil; M would read them through, mark the passages he needed and dictate these to his secretary, subsequently destroying the originals.

Churchill, of course, had been appointed Prime Minister on 10 May and just a month later, on 10 June, he dismissed

Sir Vernon Kell ('Your precious Winston has sacked the General,' was Lady Kell's outraged comment, delivered to the staff at Wormwood Scrubs where she managed the canteen); the post of Director-General was temporarily filled by Brigadier Harker, who was promoted to Deputy DG, and then by Sir David Petrie who took it over in November 1940. Guy Liddel replaced Brigadier Harker as Director of 'B' Division. M, who'd been recruited and trained by Kell, naturally felt indignant about his dismissal, as many of us were (though he got on well with both of Kell's successors) – and indeed, after this, I think in some respects M's abilities were underestimated by Head Office; certainly a number of his reports on the subject of Communist infiltration never received the attention they deserved.

It infuriated M when his assessments of a situation were dismissed as unimportant by people who ought to have known better. One of his papers, for example, entitled 'The Comintern is not Dead', predicted with great accuracy the developments in Russia's policy with regard to Britain after the war, as well as underscoring the harmful character of her current subversionary activities. Roger Hollis, to whom the paper was first submitted, sent it back with the comment that it was over-theoretical. It then went to Guy Liddell and various other Soviet-experts, all of whom expressed the opinion that M was allowing his personal distaste for Communism to swamp his judgement. M, undaunted, got the paper off to Desmond Morton, Churchill's private secretary, who was also a personal friend of his, with the plea that it should be passed on to the Prime Minister. (Other matters about which M felt strongly were communicated to Churchill in this way, sometimes to good effect, and always so tactfully that the source of the information was never disclosed.) Desmond Morton – later Sir Desmond – did his best for M, persuading Churchill to read the paper (as everyone now knows, the 'old man' was very difficult to work for), but his efforts came to nothing as the Prime Minister was then in love with the whole concept of his Russian allies. M, I think, eventually tore up the paper in disgust – but the fact remains that he was right and everyone else wrong.

When his expertise was disregarded in this way M would sometimes succumb to bitterness over the incompetence and stubbornness of people in high places, but I don't think it ever occurred to him to look for treachery on his own doorstep – not before 1941, at least, when the Driberg incident alerted him to the fact that a Soviet agent must be at work inside the Security Service. Driberg's code name was M8, and one of his reports for M, which contained a reference to a book he had written, was read by some unauthorized person who recognized the allusion and immediately identified M8 as Driberg – it emerged in 1963 that this person was Anthony Blunt, ex-personal assistant to Guy Liddell and still a prominent member of 'B' Division at this time. I am sure M never suspected Blunt, which is rather odd really, as he had had several protégés at Cambridge before the war, and certainly knew all about the Apostles.* Of course, under Sir Vernon Kell, we were all encouraged to think of the office as a kind of extended family, with loyalty as the number one requirement. In my early days at MI5, I was happy to go along with this. At my age, too, and with all the Kiplingesque ideals I'd grown up with, it was natural for me to attribute absolute integrity to everyone in a position of trust in the office. There was an element of naïvety in this attitude, of course, which certainly didn't come into it with M. I think he probably just found it necessary, and salutary, to regard the office as sacrosanct.

---

* No one, indeed, has come up with a satisfactory explanation of how Blunt came to be recruited into MI5, after being dismissed from the Manley staff course for budding intelligence officers because he had been so far to the Left at Cambridge.

Kell understood and appreciated him, and after Kell's departure, as I've said, it became more difficult for M to make his presence felt outside his own department. You needed to work with him at close quarters in order to experience the full effect of his magnetic personality: we in B5(b) were all under his spell, but, with his individual way of going about things, he was capable of arousing antagonism. M's attitude to paper-work was representative of his general disinclination to involve himself in the trappings of bureaucracy. There was always something rather dashing, in an old-fashioned way, about his approach to security matters.

The Communist threat was something about which M felt very deeply indeed; his views on this subject, you might say, amounted almost to an obsession. He was equally adamant in his aversion to Jews and homosexuals, but prepared to suspend these prejudices in certain cases. 'Bloody Jews' was one of his expressions (you have only to read the popular novels of the period – thrillers in particular – to understand just how widespread this particular prejudice was); yet he liked and admired Lord Rothschild who, at the time, was attached to the section of 'B' which dealt with counter-espionage, and was rather left-wing, in a rich kind of way.

One of M's secretaries – being an innocent, as we all were in those days – came to me for advice on one occasion when Victor Rothschild invited her to tea. 'What shall I do?' she asked. I had to laugh. 'For God's sake, girl,' I said, thinking, well, who's going to miss tea at the Ritz? Next morning she announced, 'I ended up in his suite;' however, nothing very dramatic happened to her there. I think he gave her a small ring but only as a token of friendship – that was all. Victor Rothschild was something of a figure of fun, very dumpy and round, and before the war he had suffered greatly from the attention of practical jokers; he used to drive down to the South of France, I remember, and the great thing was to stick a potato up the exhaust pipe of his Bentley – he had a rotten time in those days. But all that ended when he joined MI5, where he succeeded in impressing everyone he worked with; M wasn't alone in his admiration of Victor.

M never allowed his prejudices to interfere with his appreciation of the work done for us by a couple of highly valued agents, one homosexual and the other Jewish; as I've said, his intolerant attitude wasn't altogether consistent. Partly because of this, and also because he would sometimes pretend to be parodying himself, I never saw anything particularly outrageous in the way he kept referring to these *bêtes noirs*. Everyone, I reasoned, had a topic on which they were liable to become unreasonable.

Our domestic life soon acquired an agreeable pattern; only the problem of our unsatisfactory love life continued to worry and plague us. (This was made worse for me by the fact that there was no one with whom I could have discussed it, even if pride hadn't obliged me to suffer uncomplainingly.)

This part of our lives did not work, and I was losing faith that it ever would. Fortunately there was plenty to take our minds off this distressing subject. We used to spend as much time as possible at Camberley, sharing the house (briefly in some cases) with a succession of more or less endearing animals. First there were Ben, a springer spaniel whose master had been killed in action, and Moth, a labrador given to me by Tony Gilson. These were both gun-dogs, and expected their days out in the field; whenever we had a free Saturday we would bundle them into a car (one of the office cars, and as neither of us could drive at this time we needed a chauffeur as well) and set off in pursuit of moorhens and other wild fowl, furnished with suitable guns from M's arsenal. These shooting expeditions were thoroughly relished by both dogs.

Next, M presented me with a Himalayan monkey which was rather more exacting in its requirements. This little creature slept in the conservatory, wrapped in a baby blanket and nursing a hot-water bottle. Ructions ensued if I forgot the bottle. Unfortunately he wasn't house-trained and this, together with the perpetual complaints from visitors he had bitten, and the broken china I had to pick up whenever he flew into a tantrum, made me feel quite relieved when someone offered to adopt him. It was a builder, employed by us to do some work on the house, who fell in love with the monkey in the most extraordinary way, eventually constructing a house for it in his backyard, and carrying it affectionately about with him on his bicycle.

Then there was Gloria. M looked up from his *Times* one morning, shortly after the departure of the monkey, and announced it was time I had another animal. Since I had practically ruined my back helping him to build a hen–house two days earlier, I didn't go out of my way to show enthusiasm over this suggestion. I hoped he would understand, by my noncommittal attitude, that enough was enough. It didn't work. The following Friday, when I was about to start out for Camberley on my own, M let me know, in his joking way, that a birthday present was due to arrive at Paddington Station, to be picked up by me. I mentioned that it wasn't my birthday. 'Never mind,' he said, smiling. 'Have one on me.'

I left for Paddington in the office car in plenty of time to meet the train which M had specified, the four-fifteen from Bristol. The present, he told me, would be travelling in the guard's van. I was to ask for a package addressed to me personally. I found the guard unable to get into his van, from which loud growls were issuing, and the engine driver, signalman and porters who had gathered round him to offer encouragement seemed equally at a loss. I could do nothing but brazen it out. 'I believe you have something for me,' I said loudly, giving my name. They all turned to regard me with interest. The guard, who seemed a bit put out, told me my dangerous animal was keeping him from doing his work, which was to unload the van, and asked me to take it away at once. I still didn't know what it was. 'Certainly,' I said, striding towards the van and remembering how, when I was much younger, I had saved two small boys from being savaged by two Alsations. Heartened by the recollection of this feat, I confronted the very large Great Dane I found inside the guard's van with some firmness, and managed to untie her and lead her out of the station and into the car.

Attached to her collar was a label on which someone had written, 'My name is Gloria. I am eighteen months old, and I am sorry to say I came into season this morning.' As soon as I got to Camberley I had to dash across to our nearest neighbours, who kindly agreed to take charge of Ben the spaniel while Gloria's 'condition' lasted. This left me with Mr Socks, a Pekinese who had accidentally come into our lives at some point, but when I considered his size in relation to the Great Dane I decided he wasn't worth bothering about. I was wrong about this, as it turned out, for he nearly burst with frustrated passion a few days later.

As soon as I'd fed Gloria I took her with me into the study and settled down to work on some reports for M; these had got held up as a result of all the bother with the new arrival. After a few minutes the telephone rang. It was Gloria's previous owner seeking reassurance about the well-being of her late pet. I thanked her a lot for sending the dog to me in her condition, but she persisted in treating my remarks as a joke. 'She's such a dear bitch,' she said. 'So loving, as I expect you've noticed – you *must* let her sleep on your bed.'

While this conversation was going on I could hear low growls coming from the other side of the room. The dear bitch had arranged herself across the doorway, and when I tried to get past her the growls grew louder and were accompanied by snarls. It was plain to me that argument would get me nowhere. I hopped out of the study window, re-entered through the back door, spread out a rug on the kitchen floor, tiptoed back to the study and whipped open the door, to reveal Gloria still snarling in the wrong direction. I quickly attached a lead to her collar and brought her through to the kitchen, where I hoped she would settle down for the night. I went upstairs singing, 'Last Night I Slept in a Goosefeather Bed', at the same time thinking a lot of hard thoughts about Gloria's ex-owner as well as M.

It didn't take me long to realize that this beautiful animal was exceptionally stupid, and, although we managed to rub along together for a few weeks, I decided that Gloria would really be better off elsewhere. I knew if I kept her for much longer I would get fond of her, so I put an advertisement in the local newspaper at once. She went, greatly to her advantage, to a family living at Frimley Green with several acres of land.

My next dog, another present from M, was the one to which I became most attached – a minute ball of white fluff when I first saw him, he grew into a very lively and intelligent poodle, who stayed with me throughout the war, and even accompanied me to Singapore, when I went out there, some years later, to join my first husband. I could never settle on a name for him, with the result that he answered to four or five.

'The Camberley menagerie' was how one of M's friends described the set-up, not without cause.* The manager of the Zoo Department at Harrods, a Mr Bragg, was always coming up with some odd bird or animal to tempt M; a lot of these we took on for a trial period. (M once kept two white ferrets in a cage in the garden; I am sorry to say I wasn't at all dismayed when both of them escaped.) We derived a great deal of enjoyment from looking after all the pets, but there were some black moments too. A dear grey parrot, who used

---

* It struck me later on that M was always curious about animals, not fond of them; though ours, of course, were always loved sincerely by me.

to talk like mad, was found dead one morning in his cage (inferior birdseed, which was all you could get, caused the deaths of innumerable caged birds during the war years). And I remember one perfectly dreadful occasion when M used his revolver on an sick kitten. The shooting took place in the garden shed at Camberley and I was obliged to watch; this was to encourage me not to be squeamish over what M described as the most humane action in the circumstances. I had brought the kitten into the house and I loved it; I couldn't believe it was incurably ill. I can still see its face as it sat on a shelf waiting for the bullet that hit it between the eyes. Both the kitten and I were mesmerized, I think; and afterwards I was more than a little deaf for quite a while. There were no more cats after this.

I never understood why M hadn't learnt to drive; his failure to acquire this skill was especially surprising as he was greatly interested in everything mechanical; his enthusiasm for motor bicycles amounted almost to a passion. He owned several of the latter, and even gave me one as a present – a monstrous contraption which kept running away with me (fortunately there was little traffic on the roads at the time, so I managed not to cause any damage). As we began to use the Camberley house more and more, M decided it was best to employ a driver to take us to and from London.

The person who became our chauffeur was a former employee of a taxi firm used by M. Then in his early thirties, I suppose, he worked for us during the day, going home each evening to his wife at Hayes. I disliked him on sight and thoroughly mistrusted him. I think I must have communicated this feeling, for, whenever he got me in the car by myself, he would drive like a maniac, scaring me nearly to death. There was definitely a delinquent streak in the man. M, however, for some reason approved of him, but I could see only one way of making our driver's services redundant. I took myself off to the London School of Driving for a course of lessons.

After a few weeks with us, his wife left him and he acquired a girlfriend. (I got this information from M.) Whenever we had no guests staying at Camberley the two of them, and M, would go off for a spot of coarse-fishing. The catch was very welcome, of course; but all the time I was aware of some disturbing undercurrents in the atmosphere – nothing I could exactly put my finger on. My aversion grew stronger. Soon the girlfriend dropped out of the fishing trips, but this did not stop M and the chauffeur going off together. I didn't like it at all.

One of my tasks at the office was to deal with M's mail, personal and otherwise; one morning a very unusual-looking letter was amongst the ordinary typewritten envelopes in the in-tray. It was addressed in an uneducated hand to M, and when I opened it I found it had come from the chauffeur's girlfriend. 'Dear Sir,' the letter began. Now, this girl should not in any circumstances have been given the office address; how she'd come by it I do not know, but it seemed reasonable to decide that the driver was to blame. This implied that he had some sort of hold over M, who wouldn't normally have tolerated such an obvious breach of security. These thoughts came into my mind as I scanned the letter. 'Dear Sir' – and it went on, 'I have not seen "Stanley" for some time and he refuses to get in touch with me because he said due to his job you cannot allow him to see me and I am having his baby.' I got to my feet to pass this pitiful document to M who was working at his desk. His amiable expression changed to one of anger. 'What's this?' he said. 'Why has she sent the letter here? This has nothing to do with me.' And he added, 'We'll have to get rid of him. Clearly he can't be trusted, he's a security hazard.' I said nothing, but I couldn't help thinking the whole business very odd.

Fortunately my driving was improving all the time and I knew I'd soon be in a position to recommend myself to M as a replacement driver. In the meantime he continued in our employ, though I deduced from his surly demeanour that he knew his situation was insecure. It happened one evening that he was obliged to drive me down to Camberley on my own, as M was detained in London until the following day. Neither of us spoke on the journey until he suddenly announced from the front seat that he was freezing, and asked if I'd mind being taken slightly out of my way so that he might collect an overcoat from his home at Hayes. Something about this didn't ring quite true, apart from the fact that it wasn't particularly cold at the time – still, car heaters hadn't been invented then, and I couldn't disprove the assertion, so I rather grudgingly gave him permission to make the detour.

It was getting quite dark when we arrived in Hayes and drew up outside a semi-detached villa. I was invited in but said no, suddenly feeling extremely apprehensive for no good reason. In the state of unease I'd fallen into, I imagined he had taken it into his head to do me some harm. It didn't matter that I knew I was being unreasonable. Why should he bother? I asked myself. Of course he knew I was doing my best to get rid of him, but this hardly gave him an adequate incentive to act in the way I was beginning to envisage. Had his plan been to lure me into his horrible house? And why was he taking so long to collect the coat? Did he think, if he delayed long enough, impatience would drive me to follow him in?

By now I was well and truly in the grip of an irrational fear. Eventually he came out, carrying an overcoat which he didn't trouble to put on, settled himself in the driver's seat and started up the engine. I asked him to hurry, on the pretext that I was expecting some important guests. We drove in silence. In my state of mind the Camberley pine trees in the dusk produced an unbelievably sinister impression. 'Will that be all, Miss?' the chauffeur asked in his pseudo-ingratiating way. I shivered as I got out of the car but managed to say 'Goodnight' quite calmly before letting myself in and quickly sliding the bolt into place. My heart was beating ridiculously fast. It wasn't usual for me to suffer such trepidation, especially with no apparent cause. In one sense I understood how silly and nervy I'd been, but in another I couldn't so easily let go of the idea that something had been wrong. I decided not to mention the incident to anyone – there would have been no point, as I had nothing tangible to go on. Perhaps, in my mind, I associated this man with M at that particular time, and simply transferred to one – the one who didn't matter to me – the ruthlessness I'd half-consciously perceived in the other? It's impossible to say, but I know the vague panic I experienced on that occasion was far more powerful than any reasonable fear would have been.

He was sacked shortly afterwards and left, as far as I know, without causing trouble. I took over the driving, surprising M with my newly acquired competence; for some reason he hadn't expected me to make a go of it. He was generous enough to admit he'd been wrong, though, and very pleased to have me to drive him when he needed me.

A division of the main office was concerned with the planting of servants in suspect embassies, and often one of these particular recruits would be sent to us at Camberley, for preliminary vetting. We had to report on the ability of each to pass muster as a cook, butler, kitchenmaid or whatever as well as assessing the extent to which he or she could be trusted. We found the majority of these trainee agents deserved full marks for loyalty and good behaviour, but on one occasion we were landed with a tiny Hungarian virago who frightened the life out of the daily maid as well as M and myself. Hearing noises coming from the kitchen late one Saturday night, I went to investigate and discovered Maria energetically scraping the skins from a very large quantity of vegetables, surrounded with bowls and saucepans of water. 'Why are you doing this now?' I asked.

She turned round and glared at me, very small and ferocious in the vast kitchen. 'It is the custom,' she said. 'All *ladies* know that vegetables for Sunday lunch are peeled and left in water overnight. No *lady* needs to ask this question.'

'Oh,' I said; but I couldn't help adding, 'Why so many?'

'In this house,' she stated emphatically, 'in this house, one never knows how many guests will arrive for lunch.' This was true, and I was about to concede the point and go, but she hadn't finished with me. 'One thing further,' she said. 'Look at this knife, Miss Miller, please. Is it sharp? I ask, is it sharp? I cannot peel vegetables with such an implement. The cutting edge is not good, you see.' She regarded the knife as if it were a disgusting insect she'd found in her food. 'All *gentlemen's* houses have sharp knives in the kitchen.'

I reported her complaint to M in the study and we both laughed heartily. Maria disliked M; she made him nervous, and because of this he paid her no attention instead of expending a bit of charm on her which he could have done easily. 'I'll have to buy her a knife,' I said. 'Will the petty cash stand it, Max, do you think?'

There wasn't exactly an abundance of steel at the time, and knives were in rather short supply; after a lot of searching I managed to find a marvellous one but even this did not placate our irascible cook and we decided she was more trouble than she was worth. Under instruction from M, I'd become a fairly tolerable cook myself, and I had no objection to taking on this job too. (He'd begun by showing me how to tell whether or not an egg was boiled without cracking the shell – useful in wartime when everyone was rationed to an egg a week – but I'd progressed quite a bit since then.) The problem was that Maria's actual employers – who had passed her on to us while they waited to fit her into a very special slot – had no wish to have her back. 'Can't you keep her for a bit longer?' they asked M. He, however, had had enough and declined very firmly. A slight coldness ensued between us and the main office, but it soon blew over and it was worth it to get rid of our Hungarian harridan.

The vegetables Maria had prepared so assiduously were all grown by us at Camberley; as soon as rationing started to bite it became part of everyone's patriotic duty to plough up their gardens and turn elegant flower-beds into a vegetable paradise. You were expected to keep chickens too, even though the corn to feed them was difficult to come by. (There was of course a black market for everything but that had to be found and the goods paid for, often exorbitantly.) It was about this time that 'cover charges' in restaurants came in, never to disappear. This policy was initiated by Lord Woolton, the splendid Minister of Food who also devised the pie which bears his name: an excellent dish consisting of potatoes, carrots and turnips if I remember it correctly. Everyone thought well of Lord Woolton who probably saved our teeth and kept us healthy.

There was one well-known London butcher who required a tip of two shillings and sixpence for supplying his customers with black-market meat, and did an excellent trade. On one occasion I remember standing in the queue outside his shop, a half-crown ready in my hand; in front of me was a woman with a small boy who demanded, 'Mummy, why do you have to pay extra when you buy meat from this shop?' We both laughed, and she remarked ruefully, 'I wonder how we are going to bring our children up to be honest after the war when we behave like this.' Two and six was a lot of money in those days, and Henry, our obliging butcher, was able to start up a shop of his own after the war on his black-market proceeds.

The Camberley house, as our temperamental cook had observed, was a place where people kept turning up all the time; a steady stream of guests, both expected and unexpected, kept me fully occupied when I went down there. M's staff, people attached to the main office, newspaper editors, trusted agents and such like, were all frequent visitors. I remember one priceless man who came into our orbit – why, I have no idea, but he was sufficiently important to some government department to merit a car and a very pretty FANY driver. A scientist, of thirty-five years or thereabouts, he was famous for having developed an 'artificial black fog' which never quite worked. His name was Basil Stafford.

Basil required quite a lot to drink, but fortunately never became boring. I cannot imagine what we found for him – probably Cypriot sherry, in those days of scarcity, or gut-rotting wine (or perhaps we did better, M's great friend Dennis Wheatley having connections with the celebrated wine firm of Justerini and Brooks). Drink held very little interest for me, and it was only towards the end of the war that I realized how difficult it was to get. The sight of Basil weaving up the stairs to bed stays clearly in my memory, and so does his custom of leaving his shoes outside the bedroom door, forgetting he wasn't a guest in a fully staffed, pre-war house where such services as shoe-cleaning were a natural part of the arrangements. (Many years later I met his widow in Barbados – the FANY driver, Muriel – and I learnt from her that they had settled down to run a pig farm in Tobago.)

Dennis Wheatley and his wife Joan often came down to Camberley for the weekend. Early in the war, Dennis had applied for a post in the Ministry of Information, but received no reply to his letter, an oversight he put down to incompetence on the part of those appointed to select the personnel. He then went to M in the hope that a niche might be found for him in MI5; M, however, had nothing suitable to offer, and advised Dennis not to get caught up in some menial wartime occupation, but to carry on with his writing until such time as an appropriate opening should occur. In the meantime Dennis did a few small jobs for M, giving ostensible employment to a young Austrian double agent, for example; and attending cocktail parties for the purpose of keeping an eye on a mid-European peer's wife whom M believed to be a Nazi recruit. (He also wrote *The Scarlet Impostor* which bears the dedication, 'For Max'.) Eventually, towards the end of 1941, he was made a member of the Joint Planning Staff under the Minister of Defence, an appointment carrying a great deal of prestige.

Joan Wheatley, like myself, had belonged to MI5 since the outbreak of war. (She was the mother of my great friend and M's right-hand man, Bill Younger.) Her job which she'd taken over from me was to estimate the amount of petrol necessary for each official journey, and to dole it out accordingly. She worked from the main office block in St James's Street. When no outsiders were present during those weekends at Camberley, talk became fairly free, ranging from such topics as office politics to the newest proposals for the conduct of the war, their feasibility and so forth. Dennis, who never liked me, would do his best to make me feel nervous and uneasy in various small ways. 'My dear, how did you manage to make this filthy coffee?' he would ask. Or: 'The dinner really was quite good,' in a tone of surprise. (Of course it was good, as I very well knew, considering its principal ingredients: tinned egg, spam and a fragment of black market meat.) His derogatory remarks didn't bother me a great deal, I must say; I knew he was obliged to tolerate me, whatever personal antipathy I may have aroused in him, for M's sake.

The Wheatleys weren't above expressing themselves theatrically. A classic exit-line, spoken by Joan as they were about to leave us one Sunday, has always remained in my mind. 'Come along, Dennis, we'll be late for the Duchess.' This striking utterance prompted a dry aside from Charles Birkin, another of our guests that weekend: 'What Duchess?'

Charles, my ex-cell mate and friend from the Scrubs, had left the War Office by this time and enlisted as a private. He was stationed at Aldershot, in training, and whenever he could get away he would turn up at Camberley, very eager for a bath and a meal and some relaxing conversation. He told us all about his trouble with his boots. Believing that army regulation footwear would not do for feet accustomed, as his were, to the best leather and the highest standards of workmanship, he had ordered a special pair of calfskin boots from his shoemaker. However, on long route marches he found these simply weren't up to the job. There was nothing for it, once the swelling had gone down and the blisters healed, but to make the best of the army issue.

Charles had married the actress Janet Johnston and by now the couple had a baby daughter. As a temporary measure they had taken a flat above a butcher's shop directly opposite the Royal College at Sandhurst, and I often visited them there. The butcher, a kindly fellow, allowed the Birkins to keep chickens in his back yard, as well as parking the baby's pram there whenever the sun shone. One day when Janet and I were in the yard scattering handfuls of grain for the fowl, one of them suddenly dropped dead in front of us. We were rather upset, as we had become quite attached to them; we examined the dead bird closely but could find nothing visibly wrong with it. Then we left it for a while, hoping it might revive. It didn't, so we asked the butcher for a spade and buried it in the yard.

After a short time Charles rang to say he would be late that evening and Janet told him what had happened. 'Dig it up at once,' he said. So we ended up plucking the chicken and eating it for supper. Such was the food situation that this action really did not seem all that extraordinary to us.

M's Agents

COOKING, DRIVING, entertaining and working full time at the office kept me pretty well occupied and helped, no doubt, to take my mind off the very unsatisfactory love life I was lumbered with – though I remember succumbing to outbreaks of temper which I now put down to that cause. I continued to regard M with what I suppose can only be described as hero-worship, and I was committed to the task of trying to keep him well and happy, relieving him of any small troubles that cropped up in the course of our day-to-day existence. For me, it was on the whole a very rewarding and interesting period; I was glad to have a lot to do, much of it highly specialized work.

In the late summer of 1940 Britain was facing the prospect of invasion by German forces, and taking steps to ensure against a hasty surrender. Around this time, a number of enemy agents were dropped at various strategic points throughout the country, and captured fairly quickly, greatly to the benefit of British morale. Not all of these were German; there were quite a few Quislings among them, some cutting very pathetic figures indeed. They were all briefed by the Abwehr, and kitted out with essential agents' equipment, as well as sufficient cash to last for three weeks: by the end of this period, they were assured, England would have fallen and they could join up with the victorious German army. In the meantime, their task was to gather information relating to the mood of the country at large, details of towns, the identity and whereabouts of the local mayor, number of troops deployed in each particular area, and so forth.

MI5's interrogation centre – Camp 020 – was a large Victorian mansion just outside the Surrey village of Ham Common. The chief interrogators here were the senior MI5 officer Colonel Edward Hinchley-Cooke ("Hinch" for short) and an alarming Indian Army veteran known to everyone as Tin-Eye Stephens, on account of his silver-rimmed monocle.

Hitler's troops failed to arrive and quite a few bewildered foreign agents were picked up as they ran short of money. Their identity cards, too, were an obvious giveaway, the methodical Germans having assumed these to be machine-folded, while in fact they were folded by hand. This was kept a closely guarded secret. A lot of these agents, I think, were persuaded to transfer their allegiance to us without too much difficulty; their own side had let them down, and many of them, indeed, had been unwilling Nazi recruits in the first place. The running of double agents, however, was not our particular province.

It was about this time that Holloway Prison became the centre of my activities for a short period. The invasion scare had led to the rounding up of hundreds of suspected enemy aliens, and now the time had come to separate the sheep from the goats. A special wing at Holloway was reserved for those detainees who happened to be women. The ambience here was like something straight out of *Little Dorrit*. I was involved in helping to conduct the preliminary interviewing of these unfortunate women – a horrible job. My instinct, naturally, was to ensure that as many as possible should be released; some, I realized, were genuinely traitorous but most were not. A lot, moreover, had been snatched from comfortable surroundings and installed in a nightmarish place, the psychological effects of which must have been devastating.

The Prison Governor, fortunately, was an admirable woman and not at all the authoritarian figure of the popular imagination; but nothing, I think, could have made life tolerable for the wretched detainees. At the time, and later, I thought that MI5, by overreacting, had caused unnecessary suffering to many blameless foreigners, and I couldn't help feeling guilty over my own small part in the business.

I remember one poor little Hungarian girl – this description is apt, I think, even though, at the time, she was married to a peer of the realm. She was in a terrible state when I saw her, poor thing, distraught almost to the point of incoherence. Her only weaknesses, I am sure, were sex and money (politics didn't come into it); and it was her misfortune to have rotten taste in men. Her husband was virtually bankrupt by all accounts, and not much use to her or anyone else; and her boyfriend, a rich, unsavoury middle-European, had, by his questionable loyalty, caused suspicion to fall on her. He wasn't up to much as a bed-fellow either, it seemed: one item of gossip, which went the rounds of café society, concerned this lady's practice of reading the *Daily Mirror* while he made love to her. Fat, subversive and boring in bed: clearly, the rewards from associating with such a person could only be small.

As a hideaway, this ill-suited pair had a country cottage, the property of an artist; with the owner's permission, M and I made a search of the place – an episode that stays vividly in my memory. The cottage, surrounded by green hills, was secluded and peaceful; the day was fine, and the war, all of a sudden, seemed sufficiently remote to destroy any sense of urgency in what we were doing: it became a matter, once again, of prying into people's lives in an unforgiveable way. I kept quiet about my qualms of conscience; I knew what M's argument would be, and I knew he was right: it had to be done. All the same, it was very distasteful. And we found nothing more incriminating than some whips and boots for perverse erotic purposes (my view of life was being broadened all the time). No copies of the *Daily Mirror* and nothing at all suggestive of treason. We soon released our poor little peeress, though we continued to keep an eye on her, her lover, and other contacts she had in her *demi-monde* life.

Most of us in the office, I think, had a pretty good sense of what constituted honourable behaviour and what did not, and tried to act accordingly. This unofficial code of conduct, however, was sometimes transgressed. One of M's officers, I remember, was given the task of investigating a spate of seditious literature which suddenly became available on the sly. He went to work on one of the girls attached to the Communist Party headquarters at King Street, took her to bed and then informed against her when he'd found out what he wanted to know. She was taken under 18B, and soon blurted out the whole miserable story. Our man, knowing that she was married, had counted on her keeping her mouth shut for this reason. It was absolutely not done to get information out of women in the way he did. MI5's penalty for such an offence was instant dismissal – in theory at least. In fact, it would hardly have been expedient to sack an officer thoroughly conversant with the workings of the Security Service. This particular instance of shabby conduct was smoothed over, but M was furious.

Most people's perceptions are heightened in wartime, I believe, perhaps as a consequence of the unavoidable stress which puts everyone, more or less, in a keyed-up state. My own curious tendency to experience premonitions, which seems to operate only at certain times, was something of which I was conscious during this period. At the simplest level, I remember a morning when I left Camberley for London, driving alone, and picked up our next-door neighbour in the office car. Brigadier Manfred Caldwell was on his way to Italy, and I knew, with a certainty that brooked no argument, that he wouldn't come back. He had just said goodbye to his wife and three children, who all adored him. I was overcome with sadness and could barely bring myself to keep up a flow of light-hearted talk; I made the effort, though, being bound to keep my disastrous presentiment to myself. I dropped him outside his club and watched him walk across the pavement in all his military splendour. A few weeks later I heard he had been killed in action.

As a change from Camberley, M and I sometimes went down to Worplesdon to stay in a large house on the golf course there belonging to Ian Menzies (younger brother of Sir Steward Menzies, and head of MI6). The family was rich and Ian's house was pretty opulent, as I remember it, without containing a single tasteless item. When you stayed here you ceased to be aware of wartime shortages; even the servants had not been lured away to newly available jobs. Weekend parties at the house were full of Greek shipping magnates, middle-aged, lecherous and wearing pure silk shirts. Gambling for high stakes would go on after dinner – an activity in which I declined to take part. *We*, at the time, were almost back to woad, and nothing in my wardrobe was other than pre-war; you took great care of such luxuries as smart little hats, silk stockings and French gloves if you had them, making them last for years.

M, of course, was perfectly at ease in old tweeds or a dinner-jacket; I, on the other hand, felt rather daunted by the glamour of this household and tended to go into my shell when I stayed here. A few years later, I think, I could have handled the social side of things with a certain degree of panache; at the time, the sense of being slightly out of my element persisted, and this was due in part to Ian's wife Liesel, who afflicted me with nervousness, quite unintentionally, I am sure.

This exceptionally beautiful Austrian girl had arrived in London in 1937 or thereabouts; she started as an *au pair* but quickly moved on to a job at the London Casino, where she attracted a lot of attention by posing in an enormous sea shell, apparently naked, but actually wearing a kind of body stocking, and standing quite still, to comply with the law: this was as far as it was permissible to go in the interests of titillation. Shortly before war was declared, Lisi, as we called her, was joined in London by her younger sister Friedl Gartner, who eventually became a double agent working under Tar Robertson and William Luke; she did quite a few jobs for M too.

Friedl had actually been sent over as a Nazi agent, and M naturally was quick to spot the potential value of such a recruit, as well as recognizing where her real allegiance lay. The first task he set her was a fairly general one: keeping her eyes and ears open whenever she went out in the evenings. Café society, where gossip was rife, provided a good training ground for the astute agent. Friedl brought in many useful pieces of casual information largely to do with the interesting question of who was sleeping with whom, and the ways in which wartime security might thereby be affected. Ordinary senior officers, through simple openness and forthrightness, in most cases, I believe, were often not very security-minded, in spite of the enormous array of posters plastered on every available surface, some bearing jocular slogans and some in deadly earnest, urging caution and discretion on every British citizen.

Like many other effervescent Europeans, Friedl herself was continually allowing her emotions to become engaged; she 'adored' Michael, she told me, almost as soon as I met her (Michael was her name for M), but understood that she had been superseded by me, and wished to make it clear that she had no hard feelings about the matter. All charmingly candid and light hearted and not really to be taken seriously – for Friedl, falling in love was as natural and unmomentous an activity as breathing. She became my very good friend and we remained in touch after the war for many years.

Once or twice, when the party she was at proved particularly exciting or hilarious, Friedl completely forgot the curfew to which, as an enemy alien, she was still subject. Taxis, plentiful enough at the beginning of the war, had become increasingly scarce, especially when an air-raid was in progress; if you stayed out late you simply walked home. On several occasions poor Friedl was picked up by the police and bundled into a van with a lot of street-walkers. The police rule for these ladies was, I think, 'No explaining, no complaining' – and make your excuses to the Bow Street magistrate in the morning.

Whenever this happened, I was the person sent to bail Friedl out; I used to ring up a Special Branch officer called Tommy Thompson and tell him our feckless friend was in trouble again, for I knew his presence went a long way towards reassuring the Bow Street policemen that I did in fact have the authority I claimed to have. It really was necessary to dispel any doubts they might have entertained, for Friedl, after a night in the cells, looked uncommonly like a prostitute. The clothes we wore in those days were very tarty; dressed up for an evening at the Berkeley, and dirty and dishevelled into the bargain, Friedl was in no position to affect surprise over the way she'd been treated. Actually, she was able to make a good story of her prison experiences, just as she used to joke about the strict kosher life she'd been obliged to lead in Palestine, when she married into an Orthodox Jewish family. 'I can't tell you how frightful it was,' she would say, lifting her eyebrows expressively. (In spite of this, one would have thought damning, early interlude in her life, Friedl was registered with the German Embassy as a Nazi sympathizer, and had convinced the Abwehr of her loyalty to their cause.)

M's right-hand man Bill Younger was among those who fell in love with Friedl, and he was very anxious to marry her up until the point when his mother, Joan Wheatley, took a hand in the business. Bill invited his mother to lunch to consult her about an engagement ring for Friedl, and some hours later, with the crucial meal behind him, he found himself buying a string of cultured pearls instead. That was the end of the romance.

At one of the Menzies' parties, Friedl was introduced to the Yugoslav agent Dusko Popov who arrived in England at the end of 1940, briefed by the Abwehr but committed to the interests of British Intelligence. Dusko, of course, was the archetypal 'playboy' counterspy, and his exploits have been well documented.* He actually embodied the recklessness, insouciance, shrewdness, high courage and luck which so many writers of fiction have ascribed to the secret service agent.

Recruited by the Nazis, as they thought, in Belgrade, Dusko made his way to London via Lisbon, full of duplicitous intentions, and returned to the Portuguese capital on a number of occasions to report to his Abwehr controller. Here, after some time, it was suggested to him that he might enlist a couple of deputies in London, to keep things ticking over for the Nazis during his own unavoidable absences.

* His autobiography, *Spy Counterspy*, was published in 1974.

Nothing could have suited him better. MI5 quickly nominated two agents whose cover stories were made to seem unimpeachable to the Germans. One of these was Dickie Metcalfe, code-named BALLOON, about whom, as a deception tactic, it was falsely rumoured that he had been cashiered from his regiment, following some discreditable action. The other was Friedl, who by now had transferred her volatile affections to Dusko.

Friedl was given the code-name of GELATINE (a corruption of the descriptive phrase 'jolly little thing'), and detailed to supply political information to the Germans, a task she performed with great competence and keenness right up until the end of the war. She was a valuable member of Dusko Popov's 'Yugoslav ring' which carried out its complicated operations under the direction of BI(a), with J.C. Masterman and Tar Robertson's celebrated 'Twenty Committee' acting as overall controller of policy. This important body, which held weekly meetings between 1941 and 1945, was virtually responsible for determining the principles on which any efficient double-agent network must be based.* It was, for example, essential to ensure that the Germans actually received the information they expected to receive from their ostensible recruits – otherwise the value of the latter would have evaporated pretty quickly. At the same time, of course, the Abwehr had to be prevented from getting wind of anything really crucial, as far as British security was concerned. The delicate business of deciding exactly what could be leaked with impunity, and what could not, became the responsibility of Masterman's Committee, which fortunately was well equipped to bear it.

Friedl, for instance, was supplied by her case officer,

---

* The Oxford don and detective novelist J. C. Masterman has written an authoritative account of its activities, *The Double-Cross System* (1972).

William Luke, with the exact material she was to pass on to Germany; she would then draft a report in her own particular style, so as not to arouse Abwehr suspicions, while he stood over her making sure that the final version was free of errors or omissions. It was then transcribed in secret ink and duly dispatched. (The information foisted on the Germans by Britain's deception planners, as everyone knows, contributed greatly to our eventual victory. In one extreme example, as the result of an elaborate stratagem, fifteen German divisions waited fruitlessly for Allied forces to arrive at Pas-de-Calais. When Rommel expressed doubts about the location of the supposed landing, he was told sharply by Hitler that his agents' information was not to be doubted. In the meantime, the real Allied attack had taken place in Normandy.)

Dusko Popov so impressed the Germans with the work he did in England that they decided to send him to America to organize a spy-ring there. This arrangement naturally suited MI5 and MI6, as it gave them a means of controlling the information reaching Germany via the States. Before he left, Dusko spent some time with Dickie Metcalfe and Friedl, supposedly instructing them in the performance of their Abwehr duties. In his autobiography, he relates how Friedl became something of an obsession with him; but his temperament did not incline him to fidelity. I remember how dismayed she was when he failed to pick up the liaison after his return from the States.

The Yugoslav Ring was eventually broken up when one of its members, Dusko's friend Johann Jebsen (code-named ARTIST), was arrested by the Gestapo in Madrid and taken to Germany; this meant that all his associates were endangered, whether or not he succeeded in holding out against a harsh interrogation. (It is believed that he was executed by the Germans in 1945.) Friedl, however, continued to play a part in the critical business of deceiving the enemy, keeping up her communications in secret writing to the Germans.

She also went on doing the society rounds for M.

The life of an ordinary agent in wartime is hazardous enough; with a double agent, though, the psychological pressures are almost unimaginable. The need for constant alertness, unremitting duplicity, the knowledge of what is at stake and how easily one's cover may be blown – none of these is conducive to ease of mind. There's a danger of falling into a mental state akin to a kind of self-imposed schizophrenia. A steady nerve, a high degree of self-control and a relish for excitement are the characteristics required, at the very least. There is no doubt that MI5 and MI6 were exceptionally fortunate in the more high-powered of the double agents they acquired in the course of the war. Our concern, as I've said, was with ordinary agents working on home ground; just occasionally, though, as in the case of Friedl, the double-agent network overlapped with ours.

A couple of old school friends from Ödenwaldschule, a liberal establishment not far fom Heidelberg, ended up in London in 1940, working for M. One of these was Harald Kurtz who, even at fourteen, and in the face of some opposition from his family, had declined to join the Nazi Youth Movement. (The family was divided on the issue of Nazism; one of Harald's brothers went on to serve with the Luftwaffe, eventually being shot down over London, and the other, a Jesuit priest, remained an ardent supporter of the German cause.) Harald came to England just before the war, and managed to stay on in this country. His family connections were good, and through Lord Robert Cecil's sister in particular, I believe, he was put in touch with the office and enlisted as an agent. Like Friedl, he was provided with temporary employment as a research assistant at the same time, working for the author Christopher Sykes.

As a non-Jewish German refugee, it was easy for him to take on the role of a Nazi sympathizer, and quite a few suspicious characters were identified and detained as a consequence of Harald's activities. He achieved a great deal of success in various internment camps, Kampton Park, the Isle of Man, and so on, posing as an inmate but actually doing the work of a stool-pigeon. A lot of innocent foreigners, many of them long-standing residents in this country, were picked up in the invasion panic of 1940, as I've said earlier; the less fortunate among them were quickly transported to hastily constructed compounds and herded together in conditions of unrelieved grimness. Much of this was unnecessary, and drew down a fair amount of opprobrium, from liberal sources, on the Home Office, which ordered the internment policy, and the Security Service, which carried it through. The work of an agent such as Harald at least went some way towards establishing who had been detained unjustly, and who had not.

On one occasion, I believe, Queen Mary, at the behest of her godchild Lord Robert Cecil, invited Harald to tea; unfortunately our agent was passing himself off as an internee at the time, living roughly and restrictedly in a wooden hut, and couldn't take advantage of the royal summons. When he wasn't playing this particular part, Harald stayed in London with a Madame and Miss Titoff, who kept a boarding-house in Ebury Street; his German-Jewish friend and fellow-agent, whom he had known since his early schooldays, was one of the other residents here.

This character, whom I shall call 'X', had been in England since the early thirties, his father, a judge and a man of great discernment, having seen the way things were shaping at home, and deciding his son would be better off with relatives abroad. X was duly dispatched to his uncle and aunt and finished his schooling in Surrey. (His parents themselves were lucky enough to get out of Germany shortly before war broke out; as far as I am aware, M had a hand in arranging things for them.)

At the beginning of the war X was employed in the

German section of the BBC at Bush House, and here he remained for the duration. He'd already done quite a few jobs for M when I joined B5(b), especially on the Communist side, never lapsing from the high standard of trustworthiness and efficiency MI5 expected of its agents. There was no question, with X, of M's dislike of Jews asserting itself – any more than Harald Kurtz was liable to be arraigned for his homosexuality. As I've already indicated, M was able to discard these prejudices at will. Harald certainly didn't flaunt his sexual taste but it was none the less apparent, even to someone as naive as I was – though I must say this quality of mine was fast being eradicated. M, having undertaken to fill the gaps in my education, did it thoroughly. Before I met him, my experience of vice was limited: working at Arden's, I couldn't help being aware of the gaudy Bond Street girls who paraded up and down outside Yardley's, but male tarts were something else. It was M who showed me a couple of these in the street, and explained how they used a special way of walking – like girls', only more pronounced – as an intermittent form of self-advertisement. When they weren't on the look-out for potential customers, he said, their gait was likely to be as normal as anyone else's. He spoke with extreme annoyance and contempt.

Harald's most conspicuous vice was smoking; in spite of chronic impecuniousness he was rarely seen without a cigarette in his mouth. His private affairs were marked by chaos; he was always borrowing and never out of debt. (Once, when I'd lent him my Dolphin Square flat for the night, he casually pocketed the £10 I'd left in my desk – meaning to return it, I haven't the least doubt, though he never did.) X, who didn't in the least share his friend's sexual inclinations, or his fecklessness, made it his business to look after Harald and keep him out of trouble as far as possible. Naturally he respected his friend for the stand he'd made against the Nazi regime, understanding the courage it had taken to resist every inducement to join the Party. Neither blandishment nor harassment had made a Nazi of Harald. In this matter of principle at least his conviction was unwavering.

It's difficult to understand what caused Harald to act as he did in the Benjamin Greene affair. This, over which Harald came a cropper, involved the wrongful arrest of one of the Berkhamsted Greenes, a first cousin of the novelist Graham Greene and the Director-General of the BBC, Sir Hugh Greene; and a man of confirmed pacifist views. Benjamin Greene was charged with being a fascist, on Harald's testimony, and detained in Brixton Prison until his family succeeded in extracting a reclaimer from our agent. In the ensuing court case, brought by Greene against the Security Service, Harald was named as the MI5 agent responsible for the blunder, and his cover was thereby blown. (Benjamin Greene was exonerated from blame, but MI5, too, was judged to have acted not at all irresponsibly in heeding the allegations of a trusted informant: what else, indeed, could it have done? The business, though, brought into the open the question of the motive behind each particular denunciation, and the need for a case officer to assess exactly how much an agent's wish to catch someone out in unlawful activities might contribute to his impression that he had, in fact, done so. This was an area in which M's instinct was generally flawless; I can remember no other occasion on which it let him down.)

From the beginning of 1942, as a result of this farrago, Harald's usefulness was at an end; X, on the other hand, exercised great care and discrimination in all his undertakings and remained a valued member of the office for many years after the war. He was able to go to East Germany on his own account, and not long ago he told me how sinister he found the atmosphere there: 'Darling,' he said 'they have everything but gas chambers and no doubt these will come.' Harald, who died a few years ago, eventually settled into the profession of historian and author: his biography of the Empress Eugénie was published in 1964.

Sometimes, when the pressure of work became temporarily insupportable, M and I would take a few days off. With my new driving licence, and a store of War Office petrol, we were able to go as far afield as we wished. Once, I remember, we set off from London early in the morning, in a small Morris car, and made our way slowly through the West Country heading for Lake Vyrnwy in North Wales. 'You'll love the place,' M had promised me. 'We'll have a really quiet time, just lazing about and maybe putting in a spot of fishing, now you've learnt how to cast a fly. And the hotel is really good. The owner's wife has kept it going on her own since her husband's been in the RAF.'

The journey went well to begin with. All the way through Worcestershire and Shropshire I was on familiar ground, having grown up in the West Country; once we crossed the Welsh border, however, I lost my bearings. To stop Hitler's troops having an easy time of it when they marched through the country, every signpost had been taken away or swivelled on its pole to give the wrong impression. This was part of a government order which also forbade locals to point anyone in the direction they wanted to go. At the first cross-roads we came to, we drew up by the roadside and sat in the car poring over a map; this made us objects of grave suspicion in the eyes of several old Welsh farmers, all armed with pitchforks which they carried across their shoulders, and accompanied by unfriendly looking collie dogs, who wandered over to see exactly what we were up to. It didn't improve matters when we made a hash of pronouncing the local place-names. The attitude of these stalwart old Welshmen was unhelpful in the extreme – they were quite right, of course, but it was rather disconcerting to be taken for a couple of fifth columnists and treated to the kind of hostile, blank-faced reception an enemy advance guard might expect. At least they drew the line at dragging us off to the nearest police station. We were allowed to go on our way and set off, blundering up one country lane and down another, until, approaching it by a circuitous route, we actually emerged at the place we were looking for. Luck had a good deal to do with this.

Another time M arranged for us to spend Christmas at a small hotel; this turned out to be The Sign of the Angel at Laycock in Wiltshire, far too close to my own home territory for comfort. I couldn't stop thinking of my grandmother and aunts not far away, and imagining the displeasure they would show, if the circumstances of my life became known to them. Their standards of propriety were pretty strict, and they would have found my behaviour unbelievable. I wore a wedding ring given to me by M, I remember, though it wasn't really necessary to do so since we were sleeping separately, in adjoining rooms. This, in fact, wasn't a suitable arrangement for a full-blooded young woman. In moments of low spirits it seemed to me I was missing out on the most obvious benefit one might expect to get from an illicit relationship, and acting in a way calculated to antagonize my family at the same time. Fortunately I wasn't often subject to such fits of despondency.

Off-stage, in Europe and further afield, major events were taking place continuously; the effect of so much war news was to deaden your ability to take it all in, with only the outstanding occurrences to act as a focus for the imagination. Everyone who lived through it, I think, remembers the circumstances in which they learnt that England was at war; the fall of France, Dunkirk, the German invasion of Russia, Pearl Harbor and the fall of Singapore – all these are landmarks in the sea of annihilation. Large-scale military disasters, on the whole, were registerd only in small ways by those who remained at home – the faces of the office girls whose marriages, perhaps, had lasted a week, when news came through of their husbands' deaths in action.

We who lived in London through the Blitz were constantly observing pathetic and heroic sights, and constantly experiencing some fresh excess of outrage; even the violently altered appearance of the city was a shock to the system. It was disorientating to find a well-known area transformed into a nightmare territory of shattered buildings, horrifying craters and acres of rubble. Places to which you had attached importance were suddenly no longer there. Eight Wren churches were destroyed in a single night. Everyone had stories of their own lucky escapes or those of friends. Many, of course, weren't lucky at all. Shelterers in the Underground were among the earliest casualties: Trafalgar Square, Bounds Green, Praed Street and Balham Stations all suffered direct hits before the end of 1940. A night-club in Leicester Square, the Café de Paris, a haunt of mine, was bombed in the spring of 1941 and turned, in seconds, from a place of gaiety to a shambles. Like Hatchetts restaurant, it was believed to be safe because it was underground.

Through it all, of course, things kept going. A milkman picking his steps across a newly ruined road, a postman collecting mail from a letter box mysteriously left intact in the middle of a wasteland – these, among other potent images, symbolized the Londoners' particular refusal to be intimidated. I know of no one who lost heart, gave way to nerves, or experienced despair. Those who suffered most, it seemed at times, gained from somewhere the hardihood to endure it. My ex-colleague John Dickson Carr, whose house was twice demolished around him, was able to joke about these experiences.

A common attitude of mind was to make light of the risk involved in any action; with time, indeed, this became instinctive. I remember when the news came through that a German rocket was about to be launched on England, and everyone believed the effect would be devastating. Someone was always on duty in the office and, when it came to my turn, I was offered the chance of evading this obligation, because of the increased danger: 'It's not improbable that you will end up as strawberry jam in the office remains.' This dire prediction made me laugh and I insisted on staying on. It wasn't until years later that it struck me how foolhardy I had been; you simply lost all sense of your own vulnerability.

Soon after acquiring my licence I became M's official driver; this was splendid for me, as I carried a document exempting me from the usual restrictions connected with motoring. 'To whom it may concern', it was headed, and went on: 'Miss X has full War Office permission to use this car. She should not be questioned on the subject as she is on War Office business. Any queries should be addressed to the Officer in Charge, Room 005, the War Office.' This gave me a free hand with the car, a privilege I sometimes abused: on a few occasions it might have been spotted outside the Berkeley, while revels were taking place inside. Once, I remember, as I emerged from the car in Berkeley Street, dressed up for an evening out, a friendly policeman demanded to know where I was going. I handed him my letter as imperiously as I could, but he wasn't taken in for a second. 'Have a good time, miss,' he said with a smile.

More often, though, I behaved patriotically and travelled about by bus or underground. This was really quite hazardous, as London, after the middle of 1942, was full of lonesome GIs and other amorous foreigners, none of them at all adept at distinguishing between a girl in evening dress and a tart. Once, on the way to a party given by a friend who worked at the American Embassy, I found myself being followed along Albermarle Street. Even when I turned in to my friend's block and clattered up the stairs noisily in my wedge-heeled shoes, the persistent person still kept behind me. It was difficult to see what he hoped to gain by this. I simply swept on, refusing to look round as he might have taken this for encouragement. He'd have to give up when I got to the door.

He didn't. 'Right,' I thought, waiting for someone to answer the bell, 'whoever you are, you are going to look pretty silly now.' However, my host, looking straight over my head, broke into a smile of welcome that wasn't directed at me. 'Bob, how splendid to see you. When did you get here? Joan, let me introduce an old friend. Bob Newman – Joan Miller.'

Bob, who'd arrived from the States only that morning, was described to me as a writer and journalist. Later, amid the usual crush and noise of a well-attended party, he sought me out and announced without preamble, 'You know, when I saw you in the street I promised myself that if you were a tart, I'd take you to bed, and if you turned out to be a guest, I'd take you to dinner. Will you come? I mean to dinner, of course.' There he stood cheerful and dishevelled, and I liked him enormously. 'Of course I will,' I said. At that point we were interrupted by people bearing down on us, full of sociable intentions, and I lost sight of Bob for quite a while. Some time later, he lurched back towards me and began to speak in a confidential whisper: 'Crossing the Atlantic, meeting you, seeing a lot of old friends, no food and lots of drink – I'm afraid all this has been too much for me. Do you know where I live? Can you forgive me, and can you take me there? You don't mind, do you? I knew you were an angel as soon as I saw you.'

From what he was able to tell me, I worked out that Bob's present place of residence was a rather smart new block of flats in Berkeley Square (the one which later housed the advertising firm of J. Walter Thompson). We set off arm in arm; poor Bob, by this stage, really needed someone to lean on. The hall porter was a crusty old fellow who gave the impression he knew all about Americans and despised their immoral ways. When I asked him for Mr. Newman's key he treated me to a scathing look. However, I was so relieved to find we were in the right place that I didn't mind. Bob's flat was on the ground floor. I unlocked the door, got him inside and led him to an armchair into which he collapsed – suffering more from exhaustion, I think, than the effects of drink. He regarded me ruefully from the depths of the chair. 'Is there anything I can get you?' I asked. 'Well,' he said, 'tomato juice would be just fine.'

I made a foray into the kitchen and found some tins in the refrigerator (evidently stocked from the PX – the American servicemen's canteen) but no tin opener. Bob, when I consulted him, came up with a number of fat-headed suggestions about ways of opening a tin without a gadget. There was nothing for it but to take the problem to the porter. This disagreeable gentleman seemed extremely chagrined to find me still fully dressed, down to my outdoor coat and hat, after twenty minutes or so in the American's flat. However, he produced the necessary implement, and I was able to open a can of tomato juice and pour the contents down Bob's throat, before setting off again to walk home in the blackout, and going supperless to bed. Bob and I became tremendous friends while he was over here, but I don't recall that he ever did take me out to dinner.

It was possible to organize an enjoyable life in spite of the Blitz, the blackout and all the other innumerable inconveniences; but work, of course, at this period took precedence over everything else. At one point I was sent by M to check the activities of a couple of Hungarian emigrés, the West End photographer Gregor Harlip and his wife. They had fallen under slight suspicion on account of a past acquaintance with the Wolkoff family. The obvious course was for me to pose as a customer.

When we looked in the petty cash box, however, we found exactly four guineas. It wasn't enough, but I took it along anyway to the Harlip studio in New Bond Street, where I told a story about wanting a photograph for my fiancé, and being unable to pay a high price. The society photographer turned out to be a delightful man, who assured me that four guineas was enough, and proceeded to take more than twenty pictures with his antique plate camera. Of course, I used the occasion to take a good look round, and put some pertinent questions to him; and I was glad to be able to report to M that Harlip and his wife were completely innocent. Most of the so-called enemy aliens *were* innocent, in fact; but because of the minority that wasn't, it was necessary to subject the lot to extensive checking.

Indeed, it wasn't only foreigners who were kept under surveillance, but their English associates as well – even pretty high-up associates. I remember one amusing episode concerning Ronald Howe – later Sir Ronald – the Deputy Assistant Commissioner of Police. Ronald was a very jolly person and a very shrewd man; however, he had a lot of girlfriends, and one in particular attracted our attention: an Austrian Jewess called Lotte Jessner. MI5 sat up and took notice: here was a security risk of the first order, with plenty of scope for seditious pillow talk.

However, as it turned out, one of our agents, who was always known as X, had a flat in Knightsbridge whose window looked directly into Lotte Jessner's window (with a bit of bomb damage in between). She was a big blonde girl, and each morning she performed elaborate exercises in her underwear, greatly to X's entertainment. He kept a close watch on her for some time, and cleared her completely of any suspicion. Of course there was nothing in it; but you simply couldn't take any chances. Incidentally, although Ronald became a close friend of mine after the war, I never could find out from him exactly why he and M disliked one another so much, as they certainly did. I don't think the Lotte Jessner business had anything to do with it, though; but, without doubt, one of them had something on the other.

The Beginning of the End

I N THE spring of 1941, the new Director General, Sir
David Petrie, brought in a business efficiency expert to
draft a report on the workings of MI5. Mr Horrocks, and
his assistant Mr Potter, from a well-known City firm, spent a
lot of time examining the structure and organization of each
department, and conducting inteviews with every MI5
employee. Naturally their activities aroused some antagonism
in the office, whose autonomy had never before been called
in question. However, the study really was necessary as the
independent functioning of every little department made it
difficult to avoid duplicating work and thereby wasting time.

When Mr Horrocks arrived in our office one morning, M

gave him a rundown of our work which actually revealed very little. Horrocks then questioned everyone in turn with regard to their working hours, special duties and so on, and finally came to me. From somewhere I found the temerity to present myself in the best possible light, pointing out that no one else of my age carried such a load of responsibility, and adding that, in my opinion, I really was due for an increase in salary. I could feel a certain amount of disapproval in the air around me as I came out with this frank statement, no one else having thought to bring up the vulgar topic of money. Mr Horrocks, however, was not at all taken aback. 'I quite see your point,' he assured me, smiling. 'We'll have to see what can be done.' A few days later, I heard that I was to be promoted to a higher rank of acting civil servant, with an accompanying pay rise; this pleased me greatly, as it hadn't been easy to speak out so brashly, and I really did think my claim was justified.

I often wondered what Mr Horrocks made of B5(b), whose security operations were naturally hedged around with deviousness and obfuscation. It's possible, indeed, that only M and perhaps Bill Younger were fully aware of the intricacies in all our dealings. No outsider could possibly hope to gain an understanding of everything we had in hand. Perhaps Mr Horrocks made allowance for this; his report certainly didn't take a critical view of M or his department. What it recommended most strongly was that care should be exercised in the matter of recruitment. Under Sir Vernon Kell, the Security Service acquired its staff through an 'old boy' network, accredited officers putting forward the names of others whose background and reliability they could vouch for. According to Kell, this made for stability within the organization, but it also, of course, meant that many employees were taken on more or less on trust.

M, along with others like Guy Liddell, Tar Robertson, Dick White and Jasper Harker, was among Kell's cherished officers, and naturally he subscribed in some measure to Kell's ideas regarding recruitment. My recommendation was sufficient, in one instance, to get a new case officer accepted into B5(b), even though his record wasn't completely spotless.

Richard Darwall, an old friend whom I hadn't seen for some time, had just been invalided out of active service as an officer with the Royal Marines when I met him in the street in 1941. He was rather at a loose end, he told me: nothing but a few photographic assignments for *Picture Post* and *Lilliput* magazines between him and boredom. Before the war, Richard had written a best-selling novel based on the life of John Mytton, the well-known sportsman and eccentric who died in 1834; but this, apparently, had exhausted his capacity for literary work. I knew that M was on the look-out for a suitable candidate to join our little office group: we were under increasing pressure as reports of incidents requiring on-the-spot investigation were coming in from all over the country. I thought I had found the right man. Richard, I knew, was both able and trustworthy. He was also enthusiastic about the idea when I put it to him; and so was M.

However, it turned out that Richard, at some time in the past, had actually managed to get himself classified as a potentially disruptive character, appearing under this heading in the office files. I was perfectly certain there was nothing in it. Richard was listed solely on account of his one-time friendship with a girl called Eve Andrews. Now Eve, as it happened, was an old friend of mine too, from my Elizabeth Arden days. I didn't for a moment take seriously the allegations against her, any more than I credited Richard with sinister intentions; I could easily understand how Eve's impetuosity might have got her into trouble, but I knew it was nothing worse than that.

Nevertheless, the fact that she'd once been considered sufficiently unsound to merit inclusion in MI5's files should have been enough to exclude Richard – her ex-boyfriend –

from the possibility of employment there. 'Right,' said M, his cigarette as usual hanging out of his mouth, 'there's only one way to deal with this.' I was used to him taking matters into his own hands, of course, ignoring the rules when they got in his way; but I didn't expect to see him tamper with the office files which I'd been taught to regard as inviolable. But there it was. He tore out the page which contained the Andrews/Darwell entry and replaced the file on the Registry shelf. The expression on my face as I watched this unlawful act simply made him smile.

M certainly never minded taking a risk, and he positively enjoyed stage-managing an audacious piece of play-acting to prove a point. The Services, for example, were extremely reluctant to accept criticism of their security measures, even when, according to our information, it was fully justified. An instance of such pig-headedness, which I remember clearly, concerned the RAF. A factory in Luton, which manufactured small arms parts for aircraft, was supposed to be heavily guarded at all times. Reports received by MI5 suggested that it wasn't. These were passed on to RAF security by the department concerned, and a high-handed reply came back at once, advising MI5 to attend to its own affairs.

This was too much for the recipient of the letter, who came to M in a state of annoyance, with the suggestion that M should intervene in the business in whatever way he saw fit. M, who was never at the loss for a colourful plan of action, was delighted with the assignment. He selected two of his colleagues, Bill Younger and another officer, both fairly inconspicuous in appearance, fitted them out with workmens overalls and sent them off to Luton to commit a burglary. It took them three days to case the factory and get the timing of their entrance right. Then, following M's instructions, they walked briskly through one of the workshops, helping themselves, on the way, to as many vital and secret small arms parts as they could carry. The shed was crowded with workers, but the MI5 men met with no kind of challenge at all, no one even required them to produce a works identity card. They returned to London in triumph with their haul, which M promptly dispatched to the appropriate department of the RAF, together with a frank account of how he'd come by it.

The RAF was furious and insisted that such behaviour was hardly playing the game. (This reaction, of course, came from the older generation of ground staff officers, not from the gallant fighter pilots whose safety depended partly on an adequate degree of secrecy being maintained.) It was, indeed, a very tricky undertaking; if we'd failed to get away with it, the office would have been embarrassed by having the matter brought up in parliament. However, in the event, the point was taken and security tightened. M, quite apart from relishing the illegal aspect of the operation, was adamant that Air Force obstinacy should not be allowed to endanger lives – this attitude was unimpeachable, of course.

There were three remote figures in the main office whom I always thought of as the three grey men: Guy Liddell, Dick White and Roger Hollis. I never knew any of them well, and I remember gaining an impression that Guy Liddell was interested in his music – he was an accomplished amateur cellist – almost to the exclusion of everything else, and that the other two were in some measure ineffectual; Dick White in particular I saw as a rather weak individual. I was wrong, of course, as his later achievements showed. I wonder if the effect they produced had an element of calculation about it: if it suited their purpose, in fact, to appear less shrewd and authoritative than they really were. When I read Chapman Pincher's interesting book, *Their Trade is Treachery*, I was greatly taken with the idea that Roger Hollis might, in fact, have been a Soviet agent – though there's plenty of evidence to the contrary, I couldn't help remembering how Hollis had been so dismissive of M's anti-Communist reports.

Throughout 1942, I was still engaged in conducting interviews with people who believed they had valuable information to offer on the subject of spies, cranks and spreaders of disaffection. One old lady, I remember, was notorious for her denunciations of all and sundry. It raised a groan or a laugh, depending on the mood you were in, whenever she summoned some security officer to listen to another of her tales. I spent one tedious afternoon at St Ermin's Hotel in Westminster with her, trying to pay proper attention to the allegations she was making against someone working at the BBC. This man, she insisted, was a Communist spy. 'Now, my dear, whatever you do, make sure you do something about him.' The evidence she offered in support of her hypothesis seemed pretty far-fetched and insubstantial to me. Nevertheless, I duly submitted my report of the interview – without, however, expecting it to produce any action on the part of MI5. (It would have been passed on to Roger Hollis.) In fact, I heard no more about the matter, and it wasn't until years later that I realized how faulty my intuition had been. The old lady, who'd cried 'Wolf' too often to be taken seriously, had indeed got hold of something authentic on this occasion. Guy Burgess was the BBC employee who'd aroused her suspicion.

M's wife Lois Knight, as I've already mentioned, had left London towards the end of 1940 to take up a post as secretary to the Chief Constable of Oxfordshire, Eric St Johnston. Eric was in possession of a pass which allowed him access to the MI5 offices at Blenheim Palace. Here, on one occasion, I met him; we were introduced by M who was obliged to make this social gesture against his inclinations. As we'd suddenly come face to face with Eric in the grounds, there was nothing else he could do. I don't know if he feared that any convergency between the different parts of his life would end in collision, or if it was just his instinct for secrecy, but it was plain that the unexpected encounter wasn't to his liking. He couldn't have been more cordial or relaxed, on the surface, but I knew him well enough to see he was taken aback. He was still in the habit of paying regular visits to Lois, about whose well-being he was concerned, and whenever he did the two would stay with Eric St Johnston and his wife. M, of course, had had marital concerns of his own which, for a long time, he succeeded in covering up. It wasn't until years later that I gained an inkling of the true state of affairs: that Lois's experience, in fact, had been identical to my own.

I learnt this from Eric St Johnston, whom I met, again accidentally, at the home of friends. We both recalled our earlier encounter at Blenheim, got on splendidly, and after this remained in touch. Some time later he described to me an incident which, he thought, took place towards the end 1942. Lois, who had come to stay with the St Johnstons on her own, seemed to be in a rather overwrought state throughout the early part of the evening. Finally, after dinner, she burst into tears and announced that she and Max were proposing to separate. 'Not that we've ever been properly married,' she sobbed. 'I know I shouldn't mention this, but I simply can't keep quiet about it any longer, I've got to tell someone. I know you'll find it hard to believe, but Max is completely impotent. Our marriage has never been consummated.' The St Johnstons, needless to say, were rather nonplussed at this unexpected disclosure; though they did their best to cheer Lois up, patting her on the back and assuring her that things would get better, they hardly knew what advice to offer her. Such a situation was entirely outside their experience.

The two young wives, Lois Knight and Joanna St Johnston, had met in 1937 while exercising their dogs in Kensington Gardens. The St Johnstons were soon invited to dinner at the Sloane Street flat and succumbed, like everyone else, to M's overpowering charm. Lois's outburst in 1942, coming as it did without any kind of warning, quite naturally distressed and shocked them. Lois remained a member of Eric's staff and was still working at the Oxfordshire Police Headquarters when he left to join the Armed Forces in 1943. Her marriage to M was eventually annulled; she remarried and had two children. The St Johnstons lost touch with her after the war, but they remained friendly with M; Eric remembers going to visit him at Frimley, where he lived after leaving MI5, and finding him on affectionate terms with a baby cuckoo. He was always very impressed by M's powers as a naturalist.

It must have been shortly before Lois inflicted her troubles on Eric and his wife that M set off for Oxford one weekend to visit her. I was staying at the Camberley house. I expected him back late on the Saturday evening, and, as I had nothing in particular to do that afternoon, I took myself off to the local cinema. It was a dull wet day and the cinema was showing a film I rather wanted to see, so I wandered along there, in a half-hearted way, to pass the time. Upstairs, directly opposite the entrance to the circle, was the tea-room. When I emerged at five o'clock, having seen the programme through, I caught sight of a familiar figure seated at one end of the tables, consuming a pot of tea and keeping a quizzical eye on the people issuing through the swing doors. It was M. 'Hello!' I said; and he got to his feet, smiling in his usual disarming way, one lip curled upwards to produce an alluring effect. 'I came to meet you,' he told me. 'I had a feeling I would find you here.'

'How very extraordinary,' I couldn't help replying with some asperity, 'considering I've never been here before and only decided to come on the spur of the moment.'

'Ah,' M said, looking at me affectionately, 'you are so close to me, my dear, my instinct tells me where you are.'

This was nonsense and we both knew it, but we left it at that.

A few weeks later he put an advertisement in the local paper that went something like this: 'Gentleman requires help

from motorcycle expert afternoons at weekends.' It was true
that he was obsessed with the things and kept three in the
barn at Camberley, including the one he'd bought for me;
still, I must say something about his sudden need to consult a
mechanic, not to mention the way he went about acquiring
one, struck me as odd. I was sure a more orthodox channel
for obtaining this service existed. However, it was probable
that M was simply acting on his belief that the most satisfactory result often came from an unconventional approach.

An applicant duly appeared one Saturday and accompanied
M to the barn where the two were closeted all afternoon. I
caught a glimpse of them as they crossed the lawn. M's
mechanic – a bus driver, I think – was a slim young man with
a nervous way of gesticulating. Whatever he was hired to do,
he did it well. M pronounced himself entirely satisfied with
the young man's competence. 'He's worked wonders,' he
said. 'A marvellous mechanic. The bikes have been
thoroughly overhauled.' The two shared an interest in dis-
mantling pieces of machinery, it seemed; the bus driver was
back the next weekend, and the one after.

This new enthusiasm of M's left me feeling rather out of
things. On the third Saturday I took a book up to my
bedroom and installed myself in the window-seat. The book
failed to grip me, however, and I simply sat there, wondering
what on earth remained to be done to the motorcycles, and
wishing I'd stayed in London, where I should have had
plenty to occupy my time. In the middle of yawning and
stretching I happened to glance out of the window, in time to
see M come up to the house to fetch something. A few
minutes later he went out again, and I watched him make his
way back towards the barn, where the bus driver was standing
in the open doorway. M had no idea he was being observed.
For the first time he was off guard, and so fell into a posture he
must have found pretty natural. I recognized it for what it
was, for he had pointed it out to me himself, when we passed

a couple of male prostitutes in the street.

As I sat there watching this avowed opponent of homosexuality mince across the lawn, a number of things became clear to me. The first of these was that I had acquired a piece of very dangerous knowledge which I had better keep to myself. M's disability with regard to performing the sexual act in the ordinary way was now explained. So was the vehemence of his prejudice against homosexuals: it was obviously to safeguard his reputation in the office that he took this stand. Not, I knew, that this need have made his attitude any less genuine, in a sense: it is perfectly possible to disapprove of something and still remain addicted to it. I understood, at least in essence, that he would have kept this sphere of his life quite separate from his work, and I don't think, indeed, he would even have been exposed to temptation in the office. His tastes obviously inclined him in the direction of what, in a phrase not then current, is known as 'rough trade'. It was plain that he'd taken himself, that time, to the cinema tea-room, instead of spending the afternoon with his wife in Oxford, in the hope of effecting a suitably scrubby pick-up.

These thoughts, of course, did not come to me in such a cold-blooded way; as I sat gazing out of the bow window, that Saturday afternoon in 1942, I was actually experiencing an extreme of outrage and unhappiness. In my mind, I convicted M of all kinds of baseness which he did not deserve to have thrust upon him. Of course it suited his purpose to surround himself with adoring women, which he never had any trouble in doing; of course the relationship he formed with me was dictated at least in part by expediency. My role was to provide a 'cover' for his shady infatuations: I was in no doubt about that. But again, this hardly affected the genuineness of his affection for me: God knows, I had enough proofs of *that*: only at that moment they were somewhat overshadowed by the discovery I'd made. I was naturally hurt by the way in which I'd been used. It was a mystery to me, in this moment of insight, how I'd managed for so long to remain in ignorance of M's true nature.

What was I to do? It came over me very forcefully that I wanted to get away from Camberley, leave the office and break off all relations with M. I knew, of course, that I couldn't do any of these things in a hurry, that I'd have to carry on for the time being as if nothing had changed. I was in a very tricky situation. I couldn't help dwelling on the things I knew about M that underlined the ruthless side of his character. I thought of his first wife's death, an obscure and sinister event as far as my knowledge of it went, tied up with M's disquieting interest in the occult. There was an un-edifying Canadian, I remember, an ex-drug addict and jailbird known to me as Frank, who'd performed some unofficial jobs for M such as getting rid of an unreliable double agent in the middle of the North Sea. It didn't cheer me to envisage this sort of end for myself. The threat of blackmail must be a constant worry for someone in M's position; once he realized he'd given himself away, he would have to take steps to destroy in advance the value of any information I might lay against him. Goodness knows what that particular exercise would entail. I was under no illusions about the strength of his feeling for me, if it had to be weighted against his own safety. It was true that I'd never given him any reason to regard me as a blackmailing adventuress, but I knew he would find it unendurable to be in another person's power, mine or anyone else's. In such a situation, he would have to gain a reciprocal hold over them.

I got through the rest of the weekend somehow. By this stage M had stopped trying to make love to me; though this was a relief, it also meant my influence with him was weakened. I suppose the relationship, in the natural course of events, would have got on to a more casual footing. Now, with my new knowledge to add to the things I'd picked up over the years, I was actually frightened of M. I had no convincing reason for staying away from Camberley the following weekend; however I invited Richard Darwall and his girlfriend from the office, Babe Holt, to join us there. It certainly lightened the atmosphere to have such a buoyant and pragmatic pair about the place. Everything went well, and from then on I always arranged to have guests at Camberley whenever M and I went down there.

However, I also had to contend with M's extra-sensory perception. I believe I possess this quality in some slight degree myself, and I am sure that in M it was quite highly developed. This made it virtually impossible to deceive him. It wasn't necessary to blurt out the truth to let him know that something had gone wrong, that a devastating change had taken place in my view of him. I am sure he understood without being told what the trouble was. How did he ever expect to get away with the game he was playing? I suppose he relied on my naïvety, and his own competence at assuming different roles, to see him through. I expect he even enjoyed seeing how far he could go, how close he could get to someone while still keeping them in ignorance of a fundamental truth about himself.

During this period we were both rather agitated and on edge. I had formed the determination to leave M, and I believe he knew it. I am certain he also sensed that something was going to happen which would make it easy for me to carry out this plan. Through my father, I learnt that my former fiancé, Tom Kinlock Jones, was back in England. Soon after this, I received a letter from Tom giving me a telephone number where I might reach him. I rang him up, and arranged to meet him for tea at my club, the Lansdowne. It was strange, after so much time, and in spite of the tears of anger which surrounded our parting, to find the old mutual attraction as strong as ever. We met again, and I told Tom my story. 'I think you had better marry me,' he said. The idea certainly appealed to me at that moment. But I couldn't think how to break the news to M.

A few weeks went past, and again I found myself staying at Camberley, with Richard and Babe acting as a buffer between me and M. M had not been well, and I think it upset him to know, as he did in some oblique way, that the satisfactory life he'd organized for himself was about to be disrupted. We all turned in early that Saturday night, perhaps because none of us was in especially high spirits. My bedroom was between the spare room where the guests slept, and M's dressing-room. In the middle of the night I was wakened by a curious noise.

I had noticed earlier that a plug was not fixed into its socket in M's room, and it sounded as if this was being dragged by its flex along the skirting board. It came into my head that M had been taken ill and was trying to attract my attention. I got out of bed and gently opened his door. He was standing by a chest of drawers in front of the window. I saw him clearly, as it was a bright moonlit night and the curtains were drawn back. He stood there so utterly motion-less that I assumed he was sleepwalking. I remembered it was supposed to be dangerous to waken a person in this state, and I glanced at the bed, wondering if I could guide him towards it without disturbing his slumber. To my amazement, there was M *in* the bed, fast asleep; and when I looked back the figure by the chest of drawers had vanished. I have since learnt that this phenomenon is known, in Theosophical circles, as 'projecting one's astral body'. At the time I was simply overwhelmed by the spookiness of the occurrence.

I was so disturbed that I couldn't sleep, and in the morning I told Richard what had happened; I was suddenly afraid I might be going a little mad, with all the strain and tension around. But this thoroughly unfanciful colleague of mine confirmed my impression that something peculiar had taken place in the night. Richard had woken suddenly as well, feeling unaccountably afraid; and although he wanted to visit the lavatory, couldn't bring himself to get out of bed and walk past the door of M's room. He and Babe made some excuse and left after lunch. 'I wish you'd come too,' Richard said to me. 'It worries me to think of you staying on here.' And Babe, who was also aware of something weird in the atmosphere, said she didn't want to visit the place again. But I assured them I'd be all right.

I stayed on because I felt I should, but the next day I suddenly announced to M that I was leaving him, as an old love of mine had returned from abroad, and we planned to get married. He subjected me to a long and curious look, half good-humoured and half severe, before telling me he'd been certain for quite a while that some such declaration was in the offing. He said he'd decided not to put any obstacles in my way. 'I don't want to lose you,' he told me. 'But of course you must go, if you've made up your mind. I shan't try to stop you.' In fact, he couldn't have behaved more reasonably or urbanely. But he added, 'I never forget or forgive anything, you know,' leaving me to interpret this cryptic statement in whatever way I saw fit. It seemed to me it contained an indirect threat.

After this weekend I went to ground for a time in my Dolphin Square flat, thinking about what I should do next. I had made up my mind to leave the office, but I knew it was going to take some time to find another job, a classified war job, that suited me as well. I talked to Mrs Brander, in the main office, the person responsible for selecting and organizing the female staff, and she agreed to let me know if anything suitable should turn up outside MI5. M knew what I was doing, and didn't try to dissuade me. In the meantime, though, we went on working together, as agreeably as ever. I stayed on in B5(b) for the rest of 1943, as it turned out, and M conducted himself, for most of this time, in an admirable manner; he even refrained from making gibes about my new life. His apparent equanimity perplexed and disturbed me, I must say; I suppose its possible that this is precisely the effect he meant it to have.

It must have been shortly after my uncanny experience at Camberley that M and I went down to Sussex and I encountered a batty woman who showed me a portrait she turned out at the instigation of her guide in the spirit world. This lady was the wife of the Chief Constable whom we'd come to see on business: someone wanted by MI5 had been spotted in the vicinity. The Chief Constable invited us home to lunch, causing his wife to start back theatrically at the sight of me. After lunch, while the men were talking, I received an explanation for this odd gesture. 'My guide in the spirit world,' she said, 'instructed me to start drawing, a thing I've never done before, having no talent for art at all, and before I knew it I'd completed a portrait of someone I'd never seen, a pretty girl. I couldn't believe my eyes when I saw you come in through the door. I recognized you at once.' She insisted on showing me the drawing, and I agreed it was a remarkable thing to have happened, while thinking the 'guide' might really have saved himself the bother of foreseeing so unimportant an event. Our hostess, however, was thrilled by her automatic drawing, and it was some time before we could get away from her.

Our next call was at Tunbridge Wells Police Station where the staff included an MI5 officer. His function, I think, was to investigate reports of Fifth Column activity. From somewhere he got hold of the idea that I would make an excellent woman police officer for the district (the first), and did his best to talk me into accepting this post – uselessly, of course, as I really couldn't see myself in the role. 'No,' I said, and went on saying it.

This was one of the two unacceptable jobs I was offered around this time. The other was more exciting, but impossible as it would have meant leaving the country and postponing or cancelling my wedding plans. An FBI representative called Hugh E. Clegg was sent over by the Americans to observe our intelligence methods. He spent a lot of time with B5(b), and I took him in hand for several days of his stay. He suggested that I should go back to the States with him where a job on his staff would be made available for me. For a day or two I was tempted, but then I remembered, having worked for capricious Americans at the Arden's before the war, how easy it was to be hired and fired within the day. I also had Tom to consider. 'I'm sorry,' I said to Mr Clegg, a splendid intelligence officer whose directness I admired. I have often wondered what the experience would have been like and faintly regretted my unadventurous decision.

In the middle of June, M invited Tom and me to dinner at Camberley. This was, of course, a magnanimous gesture on his part. It meant staying overnight, and I wasn't too keen on the idea, but, after talking it over with Tom, I made up my mind to go through with it. We got there about six o'clock on Saturday, and, after our arrival, we were all unnaturally polite to one another.

Some hours later, with nothing to foster them, my qualms began to subside. I took myself upstairs to check that everything was ready for an early start next morning. As I left the room, I caught the tail end of a remark of M's about his antique guns. I knew Tom would be glad to cast an eye over the collection. I heard the two go into the gunroom and then return to the drawing-room. Minutes later came the sound of a shot. I stood very still for a second or two, then made my way slowly down the wide staircase which was painted white and fitted with a dark red carpet. If one of them had killed the other, I decided, whichever way round it was, I would swear I never left them for a second and the thing was an accident. When I saw them sitting there, both unharmed, M with powder marks across the bridge of his nose and Tom gazing in stupefaction at the gun he held, I shouted out the first thing that came into my head: 'Are the dogs all right?' This remark somewhat broke the tension.

What had happened was this: M had carried into the drawing-room a hat box full of old guns, from which he extracted a German revolver of the First World War period for Tom to examine. The design was rather unusual and Tom regarded it with interest. On an impulse he aimed it at a tallboy in a corner of the room, and stupidly, without looking, pulled the trigger. As a Gunnery Officer he really ought to have known better. He didn't excuse his action; however, he did point out to me, later, that one really did not expect a gun in an old hat box to be loaded. This one, too, had been stored with its safety catch undone. For me, it was another of those disturbing incidents connected with M, which almost, but not quite, added up to something intelligible. Something about his nature, and the more devious of his purposes, always eluded me whenever I felt I was on the verge of grasping it.

Tom and I returned to London rather shaken. A week later, on 19 June 1943, we were married quietly. In the middle of the ceremony I allowed my thoughts to stray to the Guernsey fortune-teller who'd got it right after all, down to the detail of the missing engagement ring: not just partially right, as I used to think before my resumed association with Tom.

I sent my poodle to an aunt of mine who lived in Kent (going down there to visit aunt and dog whenever I could get away) while we looked about for a house to rent. We took one unfurnished in De Vere Gardens: gloomy but cheap. While Tom was in Devonport, waiting to be posted, I gathered together all my bits and pieces and tried to instill some comfort into the rather bleak place. The mutilated tallboy, which happened to belong to me, found its way here eventually, without, however, contributing very much in the way of cheerfulness to the atmosphere. I kept it for the time being, but finally sold it in 1949, because it still gave me a creepy feeling whenever I caught sight of the bullet hole.

The occasion of the accidental shooting was the last time I ever went to Camberley. The house was given up and M returned full-time to his flat in Dolphin Square. I am sure our estrangement, on whatever level it took place, or was observed, was the subject of a good deal of gossip in the office where the mechanics of finding things out were pretty thoroughly understood. Still, everyone behaved tactfully in our presence, subjecting us neither to solicitous enquiries nor embarrassing insinuations. M and I were accepted as colleagues, just as before we'd been taken for lovers, with only a slight shift in attitude to let us know the change had been registered.

Once my fear of M began to recede, it was replaced by renewed concern for his well-being. The emotions he aroused in me were as complicated, and as liable to fluctuation, as ever. At times he filled me with trepidation, at others with carefree high spirits. I loathed the deception he had practised on me yet admired the way he had carried it off. He intrigued and exasperated me. The more questionable of his activities made me shudder while his intelligence work commanded my deepest respect. His versatility was a cause for wonder. His esoteric interests consorted ill with his urbanity. You could say his flair for espionage was all of a piece with his feeling for the occult and his clandestine sexual leanings. But this, his darker side, was only a part of the picture. It was difficult to decide which was more characteristic of him, unscrupulousness or integrity.

It is odd to feel protective towards someone who is holding an implicit threat, or counter-threat, over your head; by now, however, I was so bemused by M that I never noticed any contradiction between my two states of mind: anxiety on his behalf and unease on my own. M, if only he'd known it, was never in any danger of having his scandalous secret exposed by me; self-interest would have kept me quiet, even if it hadn't been true – as it was – that I had no wish to cause trouble for him in any way. (Homosexuality, of course, was an offence punishable by law at the time; and he'd have been finished at the War Office if the slightest suspicion of this tendency in him had become current.) I couldn't make this plain to him, though, without coming out in the open and telling him what I'd guessed. And I felt safer while a doubt remained in his mind. So there we were, each of us wondering, I am sure, what diabolical plans the other had laid, and at the same time, getting on with our daily business in the most affable way.

I did have a scheme afoot, but it was a benevolent one. Having deprived M of my own personal services, I felt obliged to get him a replacement, if it could be done. There was one girl, very attractive, working in the Registry at Blenheim, whom I'd singled out as a possible companion for M. Her name was Suzie, and through the usual channels of gossip and innuendo, I happened to know quite a bit about her. M, to account for his impotence, used to hint at a distressing sexual episode in his past. Something of this sort had happened to Suzie too, in the course of an affair with one of our overseas agents. The details weren't known to me, but the gist of the incident was, and the point was that it had afflicted her with an utter distaste for sex. I couldn't help thinking that here was a good basis for forming a relationship with M. The inclinations of the two would coincide, so to speak.

One afternoon, as luck would have it, Suzie was due to arrive at the office with some files specially requested from the Registry at Blenheim. I arranged to be out on a job, and asked M if he'd mind being particularly nice to Suzie, an attractive girl whom some absolute stinker had treated appallingly. When I saw him the next day he confided to me how much he'd liked her. It appeared the two had got to know one another over coffee and cakes in the Dolphin Square restaurant. I was delighted. My plan, in fact, succeeded beyond my wildest expectations: Suzie eventually became M's third wife and stayed married to him until he died. By a further irony, shortly after meeting M she conceived a dislike of *me* – no doubt because there were many reminders, about the place, of my relationship with M. Because of this, I saw very little of her from then on. One or two rather tense little dinner parties, after she and M were married, and before the end of the war, are the only social occasions I remember in which Suzie Knight was concerned.

On 20 July 1943 Tom left for Rosyth in Scotland and HMS *London*. That weekend I stayed with the Birkins, who were now at Ashford in Kent, and they helped to raise my very low spirits after saying goodbye to Tom. Back in London, on the advice of a friend, I decided to advertise for a paying guest. In this way I acquired as a lodger a Canadian Forces driver called Nicki Cutts. To her friends she was known as Cami. She caused no problems at first, staying out a lot and generally making herself as unobtrusive as possible. These are excellent qualities in a lodger, and we got on well.

Then, in September, Tom came home on leave. Nicki no sooner set eyes on him than she fell into a state of unrequited passion. Tom became the unattainable love object in her life. Instead of a brisk lodger we now had a large girl mooning about the place. Tom gave her no encouragement at all, but she attached herself to him with singular determination, bounding about after him like a great Newfoundland dog. To get a rest from her we had to take to our bed; I do admit that was no hardship.

Nicki's behaviour deteriorated even further after Tom's leave had come to an end. Sighs, sulks and rudeness were all I got from her. When I reprimanded her, she turned on me a look of theatrical misery and announced in a loud defiant voice, 'I suppose you know I've fallen in love with your husband.'

'My dear girl, you've made that perfectly obvious.'

This home truth didn't please her, for she then remarked spitefully, 'He's far too good for you, you know.' I nearly commended her on her talent for repartee, but decided she was too far gone in self-absorption to understand the point of the comment. I could tell Nicki was enjoying her gloom; but I was damned if I was going to let her inflict it on me for very much longer. Things came to a head when she developed a habit of following me about the house in the evening, pulling back the blackout curtains as soon as I'd drawn them. Heavy penalties were incurred by anyone who showed the least chink of light; as it was my house, of course, I would get the blame and the fine.

When I demanded an explanation for this petty annoyance, Nicki came out with some juvenile remarks: 'I don't care if we *are* bombed out,' she said. 'What does it matter? I'd sooner be dead. God, I hate the bloody British.' By now I had had enough: next morning I arranged for the light and heating to be turned off, told the daily not to come in, locked up as much stuff as possible, and took myself off to my club, the Lansdowne. Before leaving, I instructed Nicki to be out of the house within three days. It worked. When I came back I found she had gone. I looked for rude messages in unlikely places, but there was nothing. That was my only experience of having a lodger.

Tom came back on leave shortly before Christmas and I arranged to take six weeks off work. This was his last leave before he sailed for the Pacific; it would be two years at least before I saw him again. We shut up house; I'd agreed to lend my Cornish charwoman Ethel to Joan Wheatley, leaving her money and keys, and asking her to be back with me by a particular date, and to have the house in order for my return. Then we collected the poodle from my aunt in Kent and went off to Dartmoor, staying for a few days at the Moorland

Links Hotel. Our next call was at Bath, so that Tom could meet my adorable Portuguese grandmother, five foot tall and shoe size one and a half, who dominated everyone around her.

On 23 December, Tom and I travelled north in a troop train. The only available officers' carriage, when we got to the station, was next to one occupied by a crowd of ABs; the sailors' persistent use of bad language worried Tom for the distressing effect he feared it would have on me. Actually, I was rather amused to observe how they used the four-letter words almost as a form of punctuation, robbing them of a good deal of their power to offend. Their noisy profane chatter did become a bit wearisome, though, in the course of the long night journey.

We had booked a room at the Hawes Inn, just a ferry ride away from Rosyth where Tom's ship was refitting, and we arrived at the enchanting little hotel very tired and grubby after a sleepless night. We had the poodle with us. 'You can come in,' the dour Scottish landlord told us, 'but not the dog. I've had too many dogs here messing the place up.' This was a blow. I actually had to shed some tears to get a concession: the dog might stay with me until lunchtime, but no longer. After that, I agreed, my husband would take it on board his ship. In fact, over lunch, we hit on a plan of smuggling Poodle in and out of the hotel in a squashy zip bag. He spent the nights unlawfully sleeping under my eiderdown.

On Christmas Day we had lunch on board the *London* with the Captain and his wife, an occasion I enjoyed greatly. Some time after the new year we moved to the North British Station Hotel in Edinburgh. Here, oddly enough, I met a girl I used to know well, and she involved us in a contretemps in the middle of the night. Her name was Angela, and she was expecting to be joined any moment by her husband, a submarine commander who had been on patrol. Until he turned up, she had taken a single room. He arrived very late one night and naturally made his way to his wife's room. The hotel staff got wind of this and thought some indecent goings-on were about to take place.

The house detective and the brawny night housekeeper joined forces to eject poor Angela and Douglas. Tom and I were awakened by the noise and got up to intervene. Both Angela and Douglas were a little drunk and highly indignant. It appeared there was a rule forbidding two people to occupy a single room; and double rooms were strictly reserved for those who could produce proof of identity. Our friends, just at that moment, were unable to lay their hands on the necessary documents. Finally the night manager was sent for, at our suggestion, and things were settled fairly amicably. However, as far as I was concerned, the incident confirmed an impression I'd received of the Scottish: that no national emergency could ever induce them to stop fussing over trivia and direct their energies towards more urgent matters.

Most Scottish civilians, in fact, had little direct experience of the suffering caused by the war; yet they were, it seemed to me, in the habit of taking an unendurably self-righteous tone over what they took to be unpatriotic requests. One morning, in a howling wind, I walked down Princes Street to Gieves store in search of some sock-suspenders for Tom. These objects have since become obsolete, but in the days of long wool socks they were worn by everyone, and early in 1944 you had difficulty in finding them, as elastic had become exceedingly scarce.

Gieves is an old-fashioned naval tailor's of the most sedate type, long and narrow in design and straight and narrow in atmosphere. I approached a gaunt old salesman wearing a stiff white collar. 'I'm looking for a pair of sock-suspenders,' I told him. 'My husband's at sea, and just one pair would please him so much . . .' I realized at once my appealing manner was going to get me nowhere. The look on the face of the bleak old person made it plain that he wasn't impressed.

'Don't you know there's a war on?' he asked me. For some reason I was infuriated by this stock retort.

'Do you have any relatives in the Forces?' I found myself shouting at him.

'I have not,' he replied, turning away to arrange some ties. I really let fly at him at this point. I mentioned the number of times I'd heard that particular expression, 'Don't you know there's a war on', in Edinburgh, pronounced by people who had no especial right to use it. I spoke about Scottish smugness. I think I brought up the point that those who'd escaped the worst effects of the Blitz were hardly entitled to take a critical attitude towards others who hadn't. I went all the way down the unusual length of the shop blasting off in this way, with a number of taken-aback assistants looking on. When I got outside the shop I suddenly felt much better. As far as I can remember, it was the only occasion during the war when I made a scene, and I really enjoyed it.

On my last night in Scotland, Tom and I were having a drink at the hotel bar, when an extremely nice young man came over and joined us. This was quite a usual practice for foreign and Commonwealth servicemen at a loose end, and no one thought anything of it. Archie Greenaway was a Canadian bomber pilot on his way from a base in the north to Chivener in Devon. He knew hardly anyone in England, it turned out, so Tom gave him our telephone number, inviting him to look me up if he should find himself in London. I was happy to endorse the invitation, as I liked Archie very much indeed. He was only twenty-four, but had a wife and two children, he told us, living in Montreal. A month or so later, he did get in touch with me and we became good friends. Most people writing about the war have commented on the change it brought about in social behaviour, and what a good thing this was; certainly a lot of free-and-easy friendships came into being, something that wouldn't have been possible in more hidebound times.

I left Edinburgh for London the following morning. I was in a very disconsolate state, knowing it would be two years before I saw Tom again. Even Poodle, in sympathy with my unhappiness, was uncharacteristically subdued. The journey dragged on pointlessly and interminably, it seemed. It was late in the evening when I reached De Vere Gardens and inserted the key in our front door. The condition of the house inside didn't do anything to cheer me up. There were our six-week-old breakfast dishes still on the table. Upstairs, the bed was unmade. Ethel, my charwoman, had let me down. I found a note explaining that Mrs Wheatley had offered to keep her on full time, and so she was leaving me. She returned the keys, and the money I'd given her, as she couldn't be bothered to do the work. She didn't put it quite like that, but her meaning was plain. It was the last straw. I was furious. It seemed the ultimate in shabby behaviour – not what I'd expected from either of them.

PID

ON 5 February 1944, the day after I arrived home from Scotland, I paid a visit to the main MI5 office in St James's Street and found that Mrs Brander, as I'd hoped, had been busy on my behalf. She had made an appointment for me to see a Mrs Deakin, who ran the female staff in a branch of the Foreign Office located in Bush House, where the BBC Overseas Service had allowed them some space, and Ingersoll House, on the opposite side of the road. The organization was known as PID (Political Intelligence Department.)*

* At least, this was its ostensible title. Actually PID, an official

The following day I went along to Bush House and Mrs Deakin confirmed that a job had been found for me, but seemed unwilling, or unable, to go into details about the kind of work I'd be required to do. She mentioned Sefton Delmer as the head of the department, but added that my immediate boss would probably be a Dr Derry. Further than that she wasn't prepared to go. However, she then took me along to Dr Derry's office. My putative employer proved to be a mild little man who raised no objections when I told him I needed a month to get things straight in the job I was leaving. I also wanted to find somewhere new to live; for some reason the house in De Vere Gardens had lost its charm.

With M's co-operation I managed to tie up nearly all the loose ends in B5(b) resulting from my departure. I found a flat in Hans Crescent and moved there as soon as possible. Things were taking a new and definite shape. The flat was small but I liked it. It was compact and pleasant and conveniently close to the Underground and bus services which I used to travel each day to Bush House. I started work there in an optimistic mood. However, it didn't take me long to realize I'd fallen into the wrong kind of employment. The first few days I spent at Bush House are very misty in my mind, but I know I was given some undemanding jobs; this was far worse than the transport section of MI5. I stood it for as long as I could and then appealed to Dr Derry. 'Quite frankly,' I said, 'I don't want to push myself in any way, but I have been used to taking quite a lot of responsibility over the

department of the Foreign Office, was closed in 1943; PWE (Political Warfare Executive), a secret wartime organization mainly concerned with propaganda broadcasts and other forms of deception directed at Germany and countries under German occupation, continued to operate under the PID label. (See Ellic Howe, *The Black Game.*)

last few years.' He promised to see what he could do.

A few days later I was transferred to another department and installed in an office with an ex-bank manager and a Major. It was definitely a move in the right direction. To this office came all the top-secret cables, already decoded; our job was to read each one and send it on to the correct destination – heaven help you if you got this wrong. It was necessary to be fairly knowledgeable about the War Office, Foreign Office and Special Operations Executive, and the separate responsibilities of each. To ensure that complete secrecy was maintained, we locked our door while we dealt with each batch of cables as it came in.

The Major was then in his early thirties, I suppose, dark haired and rather intense in manner. I remember he began quite early on to quiz me about my salary, trying to induce in me a sense of grievance over the fact that Lady So-and-so was being paid rather more than I was, for doing less exacting work. He held this to be a misplaced form of deference paid to her title. 'You ought to complain,' he advised me. I told him I was quite satisfied with what I was getting, and added that there were reasons, other than snobbery, why this person was on a higher salary scale. She was at least fifteen years my senior, for a start. I also mentioned that she happened to be an old friend of mine, and that I wasn't in the least put out by her earning power. It did no good – he continued to harp on the subject.

A lot of our cables or signals were coming in from the Middle East, and I couldn't help noticing that whenever one of these was included in the Major's bunch, he jotted down the information it contained on a separate piece of paper. This struck me as curious, but being new to the job I concluded that it was part of his system to keep a record of where his cables had gone until the end of the day, so that there might be no argument if anything went wrong in our office. Something, however, kept me from asking him if this was standard practice, or from mentioning the matter to the bank manager; I had discovered early on that the bank manager was a trusting soul, inappropriate though it was in relation to his peace time occupation. I watched the Major for two weeks and then I rang M. 'There's something I'd like to talk to you about.'

He suggested lunch at the Sloane Court Hotel and I went along there convinced I had got hold of something that needed looking into. I was puzzled, however, by the Major's extraordinary carelessness; he never attempted to hide what he was doing. Was he just over-confident, or had I got things completely wrong? I hoped I wasn't, at this late stage, starting to imagine myself surrounded by spies.

I told M exactly what I had observed going on in my new office, and he agreed it was significant enough to require immediate checking. We arranged to meet again the following day. By this time M was deeply interested in the activities of the Major. References to those particular Middle Eastern cables, it turned out, had been picked up on the telephone lines from King Street, the Communist Party headquarters, as well as cropping up in the reports of several B5(b) agents on the spot. A breach of security was clearly indicated, with the PID man in the role of culprit. It was, indeed, a piece of ill-luck for the Major, who no doubt had been keeping King Street supplied with political information for some time, that the newest recruit to his office should have come directly from MI5, and be well trained in the habits of noticing and watching. I am certain he never expected a newcomer to Bush House to pay any particular attention to the selective note-making he'd undertaken on behalf of the Communist Party.

The next step, as far as M was concerned, was to catch the Major in the act of leaving the office with the scribbled notes in his pocket, and for this it was necessary to alert PID at top level. Everything went to plan: the Major was arrested outside Bush House and taken away by a couple of Special Branch officers.

I had asked M not to mention my part in the business, as I had no wish to be involved in a spy trial once again; but I think something must have leaked out, as I was subject to curious looks for some time after this event. And, as it happened, the Major escaped prosecution; it surprised me greatly to learn this fact when I questioned M about the outcome of the case. 'But he was caught red handed!' I cried. M shrugged. We were lunching once again in the Sloane Court Hotel which had become our favourite meeting place. He told me the Major had been posted to a dreary job miles away from London where he could do no harm.

It didn't seem to me an adequate punishment for someone who had been exposed as a Communist spy. I supposed this course had been decided on to save the face of someone guilty of negligence in allowing him to slip through the security net; no other explanation occurred to me. It's possible, of course, that he was treated leniently simply because his actions benefited the Russians, Britain's allies; at this time England's survival was still dependent on the military effort of the Russian army. Up until September 1944, when it became clear that the invasion of France had succeeded, we had to keep considering the possibility that the Anglo-American armies would be driven back into the Channel: in that case nothing but the Russians could have saved us.

Much later, after VE day, the Major turned up in Germany in the Control Commission; this surprised me too, though not as much as his earlier reprieve had done.

At Bush House, I often snatched a sandwich or coffee in the canteen with my German friend X, or with another of M's agents, Alexander Niven. Though they knew each other pretty well, neither was aware that the other worked for M, and I certainly never thought of enlightening them. I always remembered that I had signed the Official Secrets Act, and was careful never to divulge any information, however trivial. Alex and X worked for MI5 in completely separate fields: one amongst the Yugoslavs already in the country before war was declared (the majority of whom, in fact, were firmly on the side of Britain), and the other amongst the Communists.

Alex was himself Yugoslav, and employed by the Overseas Service of the BBC; he was also Jewish. Both he and X, in the friendliest possible way, took it on themselves to give me the low-down on the various nationalities who used the canteen at Bush House, warning me, for example, to refuse all invitations from Turks to sample their Turkish coffee. (I was constantly in receipt of such invitations, as were most young females who went out to work; my wedding ring made not a scrap of difference.) On one occasion I ignored X's advice to steer clear of a particular Romanian, and soon regretted it. He'd asked me to join him in a game of ping-pong in the room adjoining the canteen, and I agreed; if it hadn't been for the table, as well as the bat in my hand, I could have ended on the floor in an embarrassing position. However, we laughed it off and remained friends.

Tom, by this stage, had reached Australia: his letters to me had become pretty infrequent and soon stopped altogether. It was the old story. Through some quirk of character he found it impossible to go on feeling strongly about someone he wasn't constantly seeing, even when that person happened to be his wife. I had known he would gradually lose all sense of the qualities in me that had made him want to marry me – it had happened before when I was out of his orbit for more than a certain length of time. Once the letters stopped, the allowance did too, and I was obliged to live on what I earned. In those days, the wife's allowance was included in the salary paid to naval officers, who were assumed to be gentlemen enough not to pocket it for themselves.

In spite of all this, I was determined not to become vengeful and paid no attention to the declarations of love that came my way, and resisted, with more amusement than anything else, various other proposals that were put to me. My resolve, however, faltered and then failed altogether when it came to one particular person. That spring, I was introduced to a Spanish barrister who had chambers in the Temple as well as being attached in an advisory capacity to the Spanish Embassy. It was the start of what I now regard as the happiest year of my life. Juan – I shall call him Juan, though it wasn't his name – soon came to mean more to me than any other man I'd ever known. As a result of this extraordinary new attachment, I am afraid everyone, Tom included, went completely out of my mind.

It was a very strenuous as well as an enchanting time. I was in the office by nine o'clock each morning, home at six, bathed and dressed by half past seven, and then off to dinner with Juan and our friends at the Savoy; after that would come the theatre or ballet, and to round off the evening we would visit the Four Hundred or the Milroy, where Harry Roy and Paul Adams played until the early hours. I was lucky to get to bed by five a.m., and I was up again at seven forty-five and dashing off to Bush House, where I made straight for the canteen and a cup of black coffee. I learnt later that I was the subject of ribald comments made by the BBC night staff coming off duty as I arrived. As the day wore on my looks improved, I am glad to say. In the early part of the morning I sometimes got very annoyed with Juan, who would telephone around ten a.m., full of the joy of life, exclaiming about the loveliness of the weather and arranging to see me for lunch. I really disliked him for his extra hour in bed!

One morning I was summoned to Dr Derry's room and offered the job of running a brand new department with a staff of three to work under me. I accepted at once. Dr Derry, it transpired, had built up a microfilm library of newspapers from all the enemy countries, week by week. (I imagine these were procured through neutral countries, whose newspapers we also had on microfilm.) The library was chiefly intended to benefit Americans with the Allied Expeditionary Force, and to be used for propaganda purposes as well as providing essential information for agents about to be dropped abroad.

Actually, it was clear to me from the start that Dr Derry was a little nervous about the project he had initiated, and that, indeed, he wasn't quite sure what to do with his brain-child once it had been passed by the Treasury. However, I was willing to take it over and have a go at trying to make it work. I was provided with a large basement office in Ingersoll House, opposite Bush House, and here, with a staff of three hand-picked assistants, I set up shop.

The new department was organized as a library and the material was well catalogued by the time I had got my girls to work. Their names were Prue, Irene and Angela, and they were all eager and efficient. I decided to present myself as a strict disciplinarian, warning the three of them to steer clear of American servicemen who would ask them out on dates. To their amusement, I proceeded to break my own rule by agreeing to dine one evening with a large, Jewish sergeant, a baby-clothes salesman from the Bronx. He simply wore down my resistance with his politeness and affability. He really was very nice. One of my assistants was asked along too, to make up a foursome with his friend, a New York schoolteacher. As it turned out, no escorts could have been more agreeable or considerate, and after that they used to drop into the office quite regularly, bringing all kinds of goodies for the girls, soap and lipstick and stockings and so on.

The beginning of June was an exciting time: D-Day was very near, and many of one's soldier friends – Rex Whistler, Charles Birkin and dozens of others – started taking off for unknown destinations. On the evening before D-Day, a Monday, I dined at Claridge's with my old friend Morley

Aeyrst, a Canadian attached to the American Embassy, going on afterwards to his little mews house just off Farm Street. We heard our aircraft going over in successive waves and knew that this was it. It was a moment of considerable tension. I didn't go home that night; there was a spare bedroom at Morley's which I could have used, but in fact we sat up all night sipping whisky and waiting for the news which was bound to come through. In the morning I bathed, drank some coffee and headed straight for the office. The excitement was almost unbearable and so was the worry – how many of one's friends had been killed?

During the spring and summer of 1944 I went down to Kent nearly every weekend to visit my aunt and see my dog. I used to take the train to Tonbridge and bike the rest of the way, an uphill journey: my aunt's house was right out in the open countryside near Plaxtol. (She is my father's younger sister, and great fun; I have always been tremendously fond of her.) It was in her garden that she and I first saw a flying bomb (this latest assault of Hitler's was launched on England a week after D-Day, on 13 June). We had heard it as it passed directly overhead, and dashed into the garden to find out what it was. It was still making that peculiar 'rump, rump' noise and as far as I remember it had a burning red 'nose'. It looked so odd that we turned to one another and burst out laughing; then came the fearful silence, followed by a crash – fortunately on open ground some way away.

The house was directly in the path of these flying bombs. At first a barrage of balloons was put up in an effort to bring them down; this proved useless, however, and the next move was to have the bombs chased by Spitfires and shot down. This was not very successful either, until they hit on the idea of using two fighters to every buzz bomb, approaching the latter at a V angle.

It was horrid for us as we were right on target. My aunt, too, was worried that a shaken airman might appear on her doorstep to give himself up. (It didn't occur to me for some time that there was no need for her to be apprehensive on this score: flying bombs, of course, were pilotless.) Earlier in the war, she had been undecided about the correct attitude to take in such a situation, whether she should maintain an air of British contempt and hatred, or invite the young man into the kitchen for cocoa prepared by Nannie while she telephoned the police. The hypothetical question was settled, in my aunt's mind at least, one morning at Tonbridge station as we watched a group of German airmen being taken under escort to a POW camp. 'Poor things!' she said. 'They're hardly more than children.'

I quickly developed an attitude to the flying bombs which wasn't altogether rational. Because they were pilotless, I had the feeling that their course was set as soon as they set out, and that, unless I was unfortunate enough to be directly on target, I had a good chance of survival.

Many times on a Monday morning as I was bicycling into Tonbridge to catch an early train, I was forced off the road by a flying bomb and took shelter in a ditch, wet or dry, sometimes arriving at the station in a frightful mess.

One of my girls in the library became ill and had to be replaced. The new assistant was tall and willowy, with a rather beautiful face; she was also anxious to do well and quickly displayed a good grasp of our office arrangements. I was very pleased with her. One day, shortly after joining us, she asked if she might take an extra half-hour at lunch-time as she had some urgent shopping to do. I agreed. She was due back at half-past two, and I knew she wouldn't want to jeopardize the good impression she'd made by being late.

I was looking at the wall clock to check the time, which was two thirty-four, when my ears were filled with the whistling noise which warned of danger. I had heard the buzz bomb, but hadn't paid too much attention to it: several had passed overhead that morning, and there had been a number of hits nearby. You got so used to the things, you took very little notice of them. I yelled at the girls: 'All of you, under your desks – quick.' Then came a crunch and the sound of falling debris. Minutes later, when I'd gathered my wits sufficiently to look around, I saw that the office seemed to be more or less intact, but knew that we were trapped here until someone dug us out. Quite how I understood this I do not know, but it proved to be the case. Still, we were safe enough, I thought, unless the building caught fire or collapsed on top of us. I decided it would serve no purpose to tell the girls we were trapped, and instead invented an office rule about being forbidden to leave the spot, after a bomb blast, until you received the all-clear. I kept them busy clearing up the dust and rubble for the next two hours, until we were released; they stayed remarkably calm all this time, mainly, I think, because they had no idea of the carnage that had taken place outside.

We had escaped a direct hit by a matter of yards: the bomb came down in the road between Ingersoll House and Bush House, killing many people. All afternoon, of course, I had been in a state of worry about my new assistant, blaming myself for allowing her the extra half-hour, and fruitlessly deploring the fate that had brought the bomb down at that exact moment. Three minutes later, she would have been safely inside Ingersoll House, hanging her coat on her particular peg in the cloakroom and arranging herself at her desk. She was caught on the island in the middle of the road and died instantly.

Juan had a flat in Hans Crescent, just as I had: this had happened by coincidence. However, it was certainly convenient. On that dreadful occasion I went straight to his flat, after being released from Ingersoll House, to tell him about the day's disasters. Having heard the bomb go off, in the Temple he had been beside himself with worry, he told me, especially when he failed to get through to me on the telephone. It was certainly a relief to him to see me in one piece, if rather less composed than usual. He encouraged me to talk about the tragedy, which was good for me. Later that evening, as we stood by the fireplace with a couple of stiff whiskies in our hands, he suddenly ordered me to set my glass down, speaking in an uncharacteristically urgent tone. I did as he said at once. The next minute I found myself thrown to the floor with Juan on top of me. He had heard the bomb before I did. The huge window came crashing in around us, through the heavy curtains which saved us from being cut to pieces; and along with the glass came some pots of geraniums, to add a touch of farce to the event. We picked ourselves up very gingerly, stepping carefully through the debris, and went off to eat at a restaurant sufficiently far away to be unaffected by the explosion.

The bomb had fallen near Harrods; for the second time that day, I'd come within yards of a direct hit. However, such occurrences were a commonplace of the time, no more to be dwelt on than an ordinary power failure or a trivial accident. Our appetites certainly weren't affected, and neither were our spirits in any radical way. We were thankful, when we got back home, to find the bedroom undamaged; and I in particular was glad the day had ended without anything worse befalling me personally than the inconvenience of having to go to bed by torchlight.

Archie Greenaway, whom Tom and I had met in Edinburgh, had looked me up once or twice in London and then vanished from my life for a month or so. Before I had time to wonder what had become of him, though, he telephoned me and I learnt he'd been in hospital: in fact he had done one flight too many and landed up with a breakdown.

He was kicking his heels in London, he told me, so I invited him down to Kent for the weekend. On the train, I warned Archie that he really was about to come face to face with a piece of England the Americans and Canadians were fond of joking about: silver teapot, silver tray, thinly cut sandwiches, tea at four, the lot. There was just one difference: instead of a full staff we were down to Nannie. My aunt, one of the many people incapable of boiling an egg in pre-war days, had become quite good at fending for herself.

Tea was laid in the garden when we arrived that Saturday afternoon. My aunt had a visitor, a rich middle-aged unmarried friend about whom unkind jokes were made in the neighbourhood: she was said to be man-mad, and fruitlessly so. Her name was Dolly. I thought I'd better warn Archie about Dolly's reputation – we were in that kind of silly, jolly, exuberant mood when everything seems much funnier than it actually is – so I drew him to one side and told him to look out for amorous overtures.

It was a glorious day. Archie went indoors to unpack his bag, and soon rejoined us on the lawn where we sat in basket chairs waiting for Nannie to carry out the plates of sandwiches and home-made biscuits. Dolly, who was talking seriously on the subject of gardening, extracted a cigarette from the silver case she kept in her bag. Quick as a flash, Archie got out of his chair and leant across to offer her a light. At the same time he realized his fly-buttons were undone. Dolly, fortunately, appeared to notice nothing amiss, but the incident nearly put poor Archie back in the strait-jacket department. I think I behaved rather badly: I could hardly stifle the fit of laughter that overtook me at this point.

The following day I took Archie off for a long walk in the lush Kent countryside which, I felt, should have a soothing effect on his nervous system. One of my aunt's neighbours was called Peter Cazalet (trainer to the Queen Mother after the war), and, in a cottage on his estate, he had installed his old Eton tutor, Jimbo Lubbock. When we got back to my aunt's at tea-time Jimbo Lubbock was in the drawing room. Introductions were made, and then we all moved out into the garden again for tea.

Jimbo was a wonderful old man in his eighties, very garrulous and entertaining. He'd just embarked on an anecdote concerning some event he remembered taking place at Henley in 1897, when I heard a buzz bomb in the distance. Before I had time to interrupt the story, the bomb had cut out and we all heard the swishing noise which meant you had had it, or very nearly. A crash followed, very close at hand, and something came clattering down through the trees into the garden. It was a piece of the wing or some other part of the monster. We all sat in silence for a minute or two, and then my aunt suggested going to have a look at the spot where the bomb had landed in a field nearby. This we did, discussing it for a few minutes and then returning to tea. Jimbo Lubbock, panama hat on his lap and silver-headed cane by the side of his chair, continued with the story: 'Well, as I was saying, that year at Henley . . . ' Archie was greatly taken with this example of English *sang-froid;* he talked about it all the way back to London on the train, and brought it up nearly every time I saw him after that.

Of course there was a horrendous side to the incessant bombing, but, as I've said, one did one's best to ignore it. You kept yourself going in innumerable small ways. In my engagements diary for 1944 I came upon the following quotation which gives me an idea of the ploys I used to stay resolute and cheerful: 'Nothing is too bad to be incurable, too good to be hoped for; nothing too high to be attempted and nothing so precious that we cannot afford to give it away.' As I've said before, as well, the fact that the danger and the nervous strain were constant made them easier to bear, in a way; when something is unavoidable you have to learn to live with it.

One summer afternoon when the sun was shining through my office window I made up my mind to leave at four and catch an early train to Kent. There was a slow train from London Bridge which would get me to Tonbridge in time to pick up the Plaxtol bus. I found a seat in the front carriage and arranged myself as comfortably as possible (if you had any sense, you sat bolt upright in railway carriages at the time, to avoid getting nits in your hair). The fields, shimmering in the midsummer heat, promised a good harvest. Slowly we chuffed along, stopping at every station. Suddenly I was roused out of my daydreams by the man sitting next to me. 'Do you see what I see?' he asked rather quietly, speaking close to my ear. I had the window seat, and when I looked out I saw the shadow of a huge wing just above the cornfields.

The train had already slowed down as it approached Petts Wood Station and now it came to an abrupt halt, with a grinding of brakes, flinging us all out of our seats (the carriage was full). All this happened so quickly I had no chance to answer the man who had spoken to me. There followed the usual tremendous explosion, but none of us was hurt; the quick thinking of the engine driver had saved our lives. The bomb fell on Petts Wood Station, causing many casualties. The station was wrecked. I remember being stuck on the train for a long time afterwards, but probably because of delayed shock-effects, I have no recollection of getting to Tonbridge or Plaxtol that evening. The remainder of the day is a complete blank. When I read a report of the incident later, it confirmed that our escape was entirely due to the driver's quick reaction. I have kept that newspaper cutting in my prayer book ever since. I believed in a lot of things then; now, for various reasons, I have become an agnostic. However, in spite of this, I still like to think we might have had a guardian angel, that July day, over our grotty little train.

I hadn't been long at Ingersoll House before realizing that Dr Derry's pride and joy, the microfilm department, could not by any stretch of the imagination pay its way in the PID budget. I had to let him know my opinion. 'The facilities simply aren't being used to their full extent,' I told him. 'Do you think it's really worth keeping the library open? If so,' I added, 'I must point out that one sensible girl could run it perfectly well on her own.'

Dr Derry became slightly embarrassed. 'Can I rely on your discretion?' he asked me. I assured him he could, and so, with a rather dry little smile on his face, he told me how he had chivvied the Department and the Treasury into sanctioning his project, assuring them over and over again of the merits of the scheme. In the end he had got his way and the microfilm library was set up at enormous expense. 'It's rather awkward,' he explained to me. 'I can't very well go back now and confess I was wrong. You see the problem, don't you? Perhaps you wouldn't mind carrying on for a month or so, during which time I shall arrange to have the library amalgamated with some other section.'

I understood that this proposal was to save face; however, I agreed to do as Dr. Derry asked. I was quite happy with the work, I had sufficient free time, and I gave the girls their fair share too. But the incident seemed to me to typify the way so many of the departments were run; you rarely found anyone willing to come out in the open and admit that some cherished and costly undertaking had been a failure.

I carried on for two weeks or so, to enable Dr Derry to deal with the problem in his own way, but by the end of this period I had become unendurably bored. There I was, sitting in an office all day with hardly anything to do; it wasn't the kind of life I'd been used to. So back I went to my immediate boss, to ask once again for a transfer. I would leave two girls in charge, I told him, a librarian and her assistant, and everything would run as smoothly as before. This time he was willing to let me go. Two days later, I spoke to Mrs Deakin, the head of personnel, and, as a consequence of this interview, soon found myself in a different job – and as it turned out, a worse one.

I landed in 'Sir Y's' office as assistant to his secretary 'Mrs X'. Important dealings connected with SOE work went on here, I was told, but in the two weeks I spent in this job I never managed to work out exactly what these were. Sir Y had installed himself in a kind of glass cage in the middle of the office, and this was strictly private quarters with no admittance for anyone apart from Mrs X. Outside, a bevy of little girls typed busily and nervously, all of them petrified of the great man in their midst. Sir Y, whenever he emerged, strode up and down the room in a way calculated to alarm, and never smiled.

It took me two days to realize the office was run on faith and hope – faith that you'd be able to lay your hand on the document required, and hope that it had ever been filed at all. We never finished work before eight p.m., and this interfered seriously with my love life at the time. I could have borne this if the situation hadn't been caused by incompetence and nothing else.

Mrs X was lean and freckled, with faded blonde hair. She always wore a hat. One lunch-hour, when we were alone in the office, I tried to draw her into a discussion about ways of sorting out the chaos. She would have none of it. The system, she assured me in a tart manner, had been in operation for some time and worked perfectly well. It was a mystery to me how she held down the job. By now I was convinced I wouldn't be able to stick it for much longer. I talked over the problem with Juan that evening and he agreed I must get out; it was having a bad effect on my morale, he said.

I went back to the head of personnel with the news that the job had proved unsuitable. I told her I disliked it very much. 'My goodness,' she said, 'surely, with your record, it shouldn't be too difficult for you to reorganize the office and put things right?' I said there was absolutely no chance of this with Mrs X flapping about like an angry hen. I'd come clutching a lace handkerchief to dab at the corner of my eye, if it became necessary, and I did this now: 'Oh dear,' said Mrs

Deakin. 'Don't worry, we'll find something else for you.'

She then confided to me that the plan had been for me to take over the office and clear up the mess, once Mrs X had been 'promoted' to a job better suited to her capacities: this, however, I simply was not prepared to do. Mrs Deakin was a cunning old thing, and I think she'd deliberately kept me in the dark about the true state of affairs in the hope that I would set about tackling the problem off my own bat; also, of course, she must have realized that the tide of war had turned in our favour, and that it was possible the entire department would soon have to be wound up in any case.

After a lot of shifting around at PID I finally ended up in a splendid job there – helping to decide the contents of a newspaper planned by us for distribution in Germany once victory had been established. It was meant to appeal to the ordinary reader and wasn't conceived altogether as an instrument of propaganda, although that came into it to a certain extent. It was part of my work to get in to the office very early each morning, and read through the day's papers, placing a large red cross against each news item I considered both interesting for its own sake, and liable to procure a proper impression in the mind of a German reader.

At ten o'clock each morning I joined the editors or deputy editors of all the English daily newspapers who assembled round a conference table in one of the large offices to discuss the question of what should be allowed through, and what should be censored. Each editor had read his own paper and one or two of the others, presumably, but I was the only person present who had studied the lot. They were all extremely courteous to me and listened carefully while I explained my reasons for picking out certain reports, and feeling dubious about others. They all had their own ideas, of course, and these were debated freely around the table. I was never made to feel conscious of being the only woman present, and my opinions were taken seriously; but I was aware of my own limitations among all these important men of the press and I was careful not to stick my neck out. I learnt a great deal, actually, from all this reading of newspapers; it was particularly instructive to observe the different styles and different methods of reporting the same incident. (Some reports, it was plain, were a good deal more accurate than others.) The *Manchester Guardian*, for example, was straightforward and down to earth, not greatly given to frivolity or gossip.

After these meetings I went up to my current boss, a fluent German-speaker, who was ensconced in an office all by himself. (No one could have been more Prussian in appearance — down to an eye-glass and bristling eyebrows – or less so in temperament.) He and I would then set about putting the newssheet together. In the spring of 1945 we spent a lot of time going through the news reports coming in from areas taken by the British and American forces in Germany. Even in the worst days of the war, I had never doubted that we should come through in the end; now, it seemed, my faith was justified, with victory for the Allied forces assured. Things were looking better all the time. I was kept busy, and I enjoyed working with my 'Prussian' boss, whose name was Eric Fontaine.

I remember particularly the day when news came in from Belsen and Auschwitz – halfway through the Belsen report I had to leave my desk and make for the nearest lavatory where I was most awfully sick. About this time, too, a diary kept by Eva Braun was brought into the office, from which I extracted a couple of blank pages, feeling the need to have something tangibly connected with the momentous events which were taking place.

A few days later I bumped into a Romanian agent of M's, Remy Hefter, who had just returned from Germany, and joined him for lunch at the Waldorf Hotel in the Strand. He was a tall, blond, tough individual attached to the Reuters

News Agency – and a more shaken man I had never seen. I made him describe to me how it was out there, because I thought it was good for him to talk about it, and because I needed to know the truth. To read about the concentration camps was simply a nightmare; it required an actual account of the horrors from an eye-witness to make it seem real. I remember Remy repeating how ghastly the stench of the places was. Later, when the News Cinema in the Strand put on the film made at Belsen, I forced myself to go and see it, so that I should never forgive or forget. Juan could not understand this and was deeply shocked that I should find it necessary.

Victory day itself was something of an anti-climax because it was preceded by a number of false alarms, with the result that the celebrations seemed to go on for a week. My boss was one of five PID officers sent to Germany at this time; when their aircraft landed, he told me, they found a minor reception committee of German officers to meet them. Eric suddenly realized that he and his colleagues were all carrying their own bags; this, he said, made it clear to him that we had no idea how to treat the defeated Germans. He placed his bag on the tarmac, summoned a junior officer to his side and barked out in fluent German, 'Carry that.'

'Didn't you say, "Please"?' I asked him, laughing.

'My dear girl, you never say "please" to a Nazi, only "Thank you". They like being told what to do; it's in their nature to obey orders without question.' He added that, as far as he could judge, we were all set to make a mess of the peace, now that we'd won the war, claiming that few of us understood the German mentality and predicting that the defeated nation would soon be back on its feet, working hard and prospering, while we would be left holding the begging bowl. He was right, of course, but such a sentiment was out of keeping at the time with the mood of euphoria sweeping the country.

The war with Germany was over but we were still at war with the Japanese, as the Government reminded those who needed reminding; people with friends and relations in Far-Eastern prison camps were unlikely to forget this circumstance. At home, the lights were on again after six years of darkness in streets, shops and restaurants; you could sleep soundly at night with no fear of bombing. We were still severely rationed, however, and thousands remained homeless.

Three months later, in August 1945, we were all stunned by the ending of the war with Japan. That morning, I was drinking coffee at Juan's flat before leaving for work (I was still at PID). The radio was on, and the shock of the announcement which came through has fixed the details of the occasion in my mind – I have a clear image of Juan's camel-hair dressing-gown, for instance, and the rather incongruous slippers he had on. An atomic bomb, we heard, had been dropped on Hiroshima. About thirty seconds passed before either of us could speak. I thought of Pearl Harbor, the sinking of the *Prince of Wales* and all the many atrocities committed by the Japanese – now these had been paid back in full. It was a sombre moment.

My idyllic love affair was coming to an end; I couldn't withstand the pressures put on me by Juan's family to give him up. We were both married; and his family was Roman Catholic. It was explained to me that our friendship was putting his career in jeopardy. We were as much in love as ever, but in the end I became unwilling to continue the affair, since so much was at stake for Juan. It says much for the quality of our affection for one another that we have never, since those days, been out of touch; and that our respective children (his sons and daughter, and my daughter) know and understand all about their parents, and sympathize with us for having been unable to marry.

One day, around this time, I was having lunch with two

friends, both naval officers, and, on an impulse, I put to them a question concerning the whereabouts of HMS *London.* 'She's in Chatham,' one of my friends replied. Then he laughed. 'That bit of information is top secret, by the way; she only docked yesterday and Tom wouldn't have had a chance to get in touch with you yet.'

I managed to indicate to them that I wasn't at all sure he'd want to, as it was over a year since he'd bothered to write to me. 'Tell you what,' one of my friends suggested, 'if you really want to speak to him get the PID line to the Admiralty and then, in a voice of authority, ask to be put through to the *London.* Of course I shouldn't tell you this so use it carefully,' he added. The waitress, who'd come over to take our order, was probably surprised by the next remark: 'I don't know why you should want to see that stinker Tom, but if there's any way I can help I shall be only too pleased to do so.'

I acted on his suggestion that afternoon, getting through to the *London* with no trouble at all and promptly demanding, 'The Gunnery Officer, please.'

'Who wants him?'

'Admiralty,' I said; and within two minutes I was speaking to Tom. I suggested we should meet in London as soon as possible to sort things out. I spoke quite mildly, because Tom's behaviour had become unimportant to me; I'd been through so much since I last saw him that he seemed virtually a stranger.

It transpired that he had got himself into the usual muddle abroad, actually proposing marriage to an Australian girl at one point. I pieced the story together gradually, partly through Tom's adoptive mother to whom the girl had written about her troubles. A reply went back to her from this source, stating that Tom had behaved in this way fourteen times to his mother's certain knowledge, and adding that, as a matter of fact, he was married already. Finally the poor girl wrote to me; I found the whole business exasperating and distressing.

Tom kept urging me to give our marriage another try, and I finally agreed, being too distressed about Juan and the end of our affair to act rationally. Whenever Tom was actually in my presence he adored me, and this was what I needed at the time. Eventually I went with him to Singapore, but my misgivings about the relationship proved to be justified, and we parted in the end.

I kept in touch with M throughout 1944, but, because I was leading such a full life, working hard and contriving to have a good deal of fun at the same time, I gradually saw less and less of him. I thought about him a lot, however; and about the curious relationship we'd had. I understood now how much I owed to him. Before I left MI5 I had returned two of his gifts, simply because I knew he set great store by them – one a rare sea-horse skeleton, said to be lucky, and the other a Rackham drawing of a widgeon ('widgeon' had been one of his pet names for me). Others I kept, and still keep, including a Georgian enamelled ring (all his presents were carefully and happily chosen). It was, of course, entirely due to him that I'd progressed from a dull job to one that could hardly have been more interesting – and everything I learnt in B5(b) had stood me in good stead. I owed to M too whatever confidence I'd acquired in my own powers of judgement and ability to see things through. We'd had some moments of remarkable accord, in the three or four years we'd spent together, as well as a fair amount of amusement and a lot of satisfaction as far as work was concerned.

M, of course, never confided completely in me and I wouldn't have expected him to: to begin with, while the danger of invasion lasted, the less I knew, in certain respects, the better. Our particular unit was known to the Abwehr and they'd have used every means at their disposal to get information out of us (I remembered the Right Club's bloodthirsty fantasy of anti-Nazis strung up from lampposts all over

Britain). M owed it to his agents to see that their interests were safeguarded to the greatest possible extent; so I was only familiar with those in whose cases I was personally involved.

However, it was a revelation to me to watch M at work; I remember how meticulously he used to conduct his interviews, the calm way he would talk round and round a subject, covering the same ground once or twice and then going on to something different, and back again, until he had got what he wanted. Sometimes it would take two or three hours, but he always got there in the end. If he started out not knowing exactly what he was looking for, which often happened in that business, it would all become clear in his mind by the time he had finished. He would sit there, smoking a cigarette, never hurrying or doing anything to unnerve the other person, just going on and on carefully in a most impressive way. I suppose you could say he was among the last of the old-fashioned professionals in intelligence work.

And then there was his ruthlessness. I've mentioned the agent of M's with whom I became friendly at Bush House, Alexander Niven. Alex decided to apply for British citizenship at the end of the war, as he wanted to go to America and there were difficulties in the way since he was Yugoslav and still officially a refugee. M, who had every reason to help him in this matter, refused to do so. Alex was understandably hurt by M's attitude and came to me. I said I'd do my best for him, but M, when I spoke to him, was adamant in his refusal to recommend Alex for naturalization.

He explained to me that Alex had let him down at one point during the war by declining to parachute into Yugoslavia, on an SOE mission, when he was asked to do so. I must say I had a certain sympathy with Alex's point of view: he was Jewish, after all; his family was pretty well known and his presence in the country would have put their lives in jeopardy; also, frankly, I don't think Alex was of the stuff of which heroes are made. I pointed all this out to M, but I couldn't persuade him to change his mind. Alex, however, succeeded in getting to the States through other influential contacts, and, when I last heard of him, many years ago, was a professor at an American university.

M was more helpful to Friedl Gartner; he and Sir Stewart Menzies between them pulled strings to enable her to marry an American diplomat in 1945 (this would otherwise have been impossible, so soon after the war, as Friedl was an enemy alien). She made an excellent diplomat's wife: I remember her telling me about her first ordeal, a huge diplomatic luncheon in Paris at which she was struck by a minor disaster. She had two front teeth on a bridge and in the course of the meal the bridge snapped – there was Friedl, anxious to impress her new husband's colleagues, and suddenly rendered incapable of speaking or eating. It was a very embarrassing moment, but she handled it with great aplomb, leaving the table and walking the length of the great dining-hall with as much composure as she could muster, and managing to get hold of a dentist before her husband had even noticed her absence. It was this quality of hers, the refusal ever to admit herself at a loss, that helped to make Friedl the first-class agent she was.

Bill Younger, under the name of William Mole, wrote a number of well-received thrillers in the fifties (*The Hammersmith Maggot* is perhaps the best known); he died in 1961. John Bingham, who eventually took over from M, also acquired quite a reputation as an author of crime and secret service novels. Recently, when he was visited by a friend of mine, he was heard to refer to me, not altogether kindly I imagine, as 'the Mata Hari of Dolphin Square'! M, after leaving MI5, went on to become a well-known radio naturalist, with a regular slot on the Home Service. Among his later protégés, appropriately enough, was John le Carré who, under his proper name of David Cornwell, illustrated one or two of M's works on natural history.

There is some evidence which suggests, to my mind, that M was being subject to blackmail in the later part of his life: why else should he have been impoverished to the extent of having to move in with his old B5(b) colleague Guy Poston and his family? He was never rich, it's true, but he always had enough to enjoy a way of life that suited him. And why did he opt for the comparative anonymity of radio work, when he'd have made such a splendid television performer? There may be some perfectly innocuous explanation, of course, but I can't help feeling that one of the risks he'd taken in his private life might have caught up with him.

Towards the end of 1945 I was summoned by M to a rendezvous at the Royal Court Hotel; though I didn't realize it, this would be the last time I was ever to see him. There, he told me quite brutally that he had taken steps to ensure that the blame for destroying the Andrews/Darwell file – an act of M's which had shocked me greatly in 1941 – would fall on me, should the matter ever be brought to light. I think I must have stared blankly at him for quite a while, as the implications of his statement sank into my mind. 'You've arranged to put the blame on *me*,' I said, to get it quite clear. 'Max, this is perfectly dreadful of you. You know it simply isn't true.'

He reminded me that his reputation was of greater consequence than mine. He assured me that, if it came to a confrontation between the two of us, his word would be accepted in preference to mine. 'Make no mistake about it.' I couldn't dispute it of course – I didn't have a leg to stand on. 'You're unimportant,' he told me bluntly. This wasn't the meeting I'd envisaged when he invited me to tea. I just looked at him in silence for a few minutes before gathering my things together and going on my way. It wasn't until much later that I began to wonder about his purpose, and decided he was taking this means of forcing discretion upon me, in case I'd got hold of some damaging truth about him, or thought I had. I was outraged and deeply hurt. As these feelings wore off, however, I tried hard, by dwelling on his actions, to gain some slight understanding of the complex drives and idiosyncracies of temperament that made M the person he was. And whenever I think of him now, it is always with gratitude and admiration.

Publishers' note

Shortly after completing this book,
Joan Miller died at her home in Malta in June 1984.